About The Author

Shaun Hummel is a Senior Network Engineer with 15+ years enterprise network planning, design and implementation experience. He has worked for various public and private companies in Canada and the United States improving infrastructure, security and network management. Author of Cisco Design Fundamentals and Cloud Design Fundamentals.

Contents

Introduction

The purpose of this book is to provide a concise Cisco IOS subject matter guide. IOS is the proprietary operating system for Cisco networking equipment. There hasn't been a lot of coverage pertaining to selection, installation and management of Cisco IOS platforms. The typical process is to select network hardware and deploy the Cisco recommended current IOS release version. Most new technical development work is with software and not hardware. In fact there is a migration toward a software based networking model that abstracts IOS from the underlying hardware.

It is becoming key for network engineers to understand all aspects of IOS management. There are a significant number of network problems that occur as a result of software bugs and suboptimal selection of IOS version. Network troubleshooting often requires working with Cisco TAC to upgrade code, feature licenses and request bug fixes. Managing Cisco IOS is complex and has a tremendous effect on network performance and availability. It isn't uncommon for Cisco developers to fix code and provide maintenance releases as problems arise.

The book provides a foundation for network engineers to optimize all aspects of IOS software management. In addition it serves as a concise easy to read guide for CCNA level engineers. IOS is a key factor that affects network design, security, support, troubleshooting and availability. My strategy for technical books has been to only include relevant real-world information that is readily available as a work reference. The information is presented and developed in layers for optimal learning. **The reader should start with Chapter 1 before proceeding to subsequent chapters.**

There is coverage of the IOS life cycle and standard naming conventions that start with Chapter 1. The selection of IOS software and code upgrade procedures are discussed with Chapter 2. The chapter wraps up with installing feature set licenses. Chapter 3 provides information pertaining to device connectivity, configuration modes and use of IOS command line interface (CLI). The remaining chapter is comprised of standard IOS configuration commands. The reader will be able to setup the switches and routers for network connectivity. In addition there are some common IOS troubleshooting techniques discussed. Chapter 4 is an IOS show command reference for management and troubleshooting purposes. Included as well are 100 CCNA questions that serve as a quiz for readers. The subject matter for the book is based on the most deployed Cisco switches and routers. That would include Cisco Catalyst series switches and Cisco ISR G2 series routers. Most of the technical coverage as a result is comprised of standard IOS and IOS-XE software platforms.

Chapter 1

IOS Architecture

IOS Software Life Cycle

The Cisco IOS life cycle describes the release data and support milestones for any new IOS major release. The IOS life cycle has an End of Life (EoL) date as well that is specified when it is released. The timelines enable customers to plan properly for new IOS upgrades and maintenance. It is similar to the life cycle for hardware. The IOS life cycle is structured with specific time frames for support milestones.

IOS 12.0 Support Milestones

The Cisco IOS software life cycle provides the time frame for IOS releases from First Customer Shipment (FCS) through End-of-Life (EoL). The life cycle specifies timelines and support activities for each major release. The following include the standard Cisco IOS 12.x support milestones.

Table 1-1 Cisco IOS 12.0 Release Version Support Milestones

Milestone	Description	Timeline
First Customer Shipment (FCS)	The formal IOS release date to customers when it is available online.	Day 0
End of Sale (EoS) Announcement	Cisco publishes notification on this day for the IOS release version and EoS (6 months from FCS.	6 months
End of Sale (EoS)	Customers can no longer order or request IOS release included with hardware shipment.	36 months
End of Software Maintenance (EoSW)	The last day for software maintenance releases or fixes for the release. The EoSW occurs 12 months from EoS date with maximum of 48 months from the FCS date. Support for release beyond this date is with a subsequent new release.	48 months
End of Security Fixes	The last day that Cisco will provide software maintenance releases for vulnerability/security issues. This date varies with the release/train. Rebuilds for vulnerabilities sometimes available after end of maintenance date.	48 months to EoL
Last Date of Support	The last day that Cisco TAC will provide service and support for the IOS release. .	EoL

There are similar life cycle support plans for hardware as well with the recommended product migration. The network engineer should consider the EoL status for all hardware and IOS software with network design.

IOS 12.0 Release Status

There is a release status assigned to each Cisco IOS software release. The release status is assigned based on features and stability. The release categories vary from IOS 12.x software releases to the newer IOS 15.x releases. The following describe the release status milestones for IOS 12 major release software.

Early Deployment (ED): maintenance build release that provide support for new features, hardware platforms or bug fixes. The minor releases are often technology train assigned as early deployment and not intended for general deployment. The ED release is only recommended where a general deployment release is not available for new hardware and/or software features requirements.

General Deployment (GD): major (mainline) release that has been tested and determined suitable for deployment anywhere. The customer surveys, customer engineer bug reports and field reports are factors that promote IOS software to GD status. The subsequent maintenance releases are assigned GD status as well.

Limited Deployment (LD) Release: assigned to a major release with the life cycle between first customer shipment (FCS) and general deployment status. The limited deployment is a maintenance release for general deployment

Deferred (DF): releases with known defects that are not available for download or suitable for deployment.

Rebuilds: quick rebuild to fix a single defect or specific problem or security vulnerability for an IOS version. Done for customers who do not want to upgrade to key infrastructure with a major release.

Interim Releases: typically weekly update of current development work. The Cisco advisory web site may list more than one possible interim to fix a problem unknown to public

Maintenance Releases: stringent testing of releases that are made available with enhancements and bug fixes. Cisco recommends upgrading to Maintenance releases where possible, over interim and rebuild releases.

IOS 15.0 Support Milestones

The support for new features, hardware and bug fixes available with Cisco IOS 12.4 and 12.4T have been consolidated into IOS 15.0 mainline software. In addition 15.0T provides support for new features and hardware. That would include Cisco 1900, 2900 and 3900 ISR series routers and IWAN features. Cisco IOS release 15 architecture is based on a single M/T train with Extended (15M) and Standard (15T) Maintenance releases. The 15M extended maintenance include bug fixes for 44 months. The 15T standard maintenance releases provide 18 month support for bug fixes.

Table 1-2 Cisco IOS 15.0 Release Version Support Milestones

Milestone	Description	Timeline
First Customer Shipment (FCS)	The formal IOS release date to customers when it is available online.	Day 0
Maintenance Deployment Point (MD)	Maintenance Deployment (MD) designated M releases are for wide deployment similar to general deployment after 3-4 maintenance rebuilds.	9 – 12 months
End of Sale (EoS)	Customers can't order or request IOS release with hardware shipment. It is 28 to 30 months after FCS date.	28 - 30 months
End of Software Maintenance (EoSW)	This is the last date that Cisco Engineering may release any final software maintenance releases or software fixes for the release. 40-42 months after FCS date	40-42 months
Last Date of Support	The last day that Cisco TAC will provide service and support for the IOS release.	**EoL**

Figure 1-1 Cisco 12.4 Migration Path to 15.0 Releases

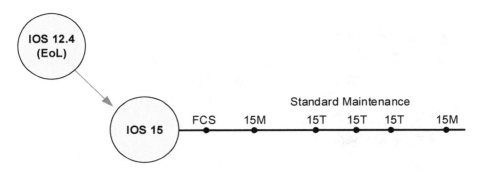

Release Status

The Limited Deployment (LD) and General Deployment (GD) release types are retired with IOS 15 releases. New releases are assigned Early Deployment (ED) or Maintenance Deployment (MD) status. The Early Deployment releases are available between maintenance releases. The MD release type is similar to the older GD from IOS 12 software. IOS 15T releases (in between 15M releases) include feature and hardware support before the next 15M release becomes available. Each 15T release receives bug-fix rebuild support for 13 months, and additional 6 months support for security/vulnerability fixes including PSIRT.

IOS Train Release

The Cisco "IOS Train" refers to feature enhancements, bug fixes and support for a hardware platform. Cisco does not recommend using IOS train releases on the production network unless the required features are not available with a mainline (major) release. The mainline release (i.e 12.3) is the most stable with only bug fixes and no features. The mainline (major) release is built from the previous train release as shown with Figure 1-2.

Figure 1-2 IOS Software Code Development Life Cycle

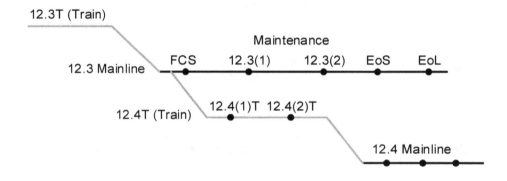

Example 1-1 Cisco IOS Train Identifiers and Hardware Platforms

M/T = 1900, 2900, 3900 ISR G2 Series Routers
SE = Catalyst 2960, 3560, 3750, 3650, 3850 Switches
SG = Catalyst 4500E Switch (Sup 6E)
XO = Catalyst 4500E Switch (Sup 7E, Sup 8E)
SY = Catalyst 6500E Series Switches
S = 7600 Series Router

IOS Platform Support

Cisco started out as a route/switch company with CatOS designed for switches and a separate IOS for routers. Cisco then started migrating campus switches to Multilayer architecture with support for both switching and routing. As a result both traditional routers and switches now deploy IOS 12.x and/or IOS 15.x release software. It is often referred to as the standard IOS platform. As newer hardware platforms were developed, specific IOS code has been written to support new architecture and features.

The IOS platform and WAN hardware supported is listed with Table 1-3. In addition Table 1-4 lists the IOS support for campus switches. Some campus switching platforms are now deployed at the internet edge. That is the result of routing and WAN interface feature support now available. The newer Metro Ethernet has promoted switches to the internet edge as well.

Table 1-3 Cisco WAN Hardware Platform Support

IOS Platform	WAN Hardware Platform
IOS	1900, 2900, 3900, 4400 ISR G2 Series Routers
IOS-XE	ASR 1000 Series Routers
IOS-XR	ASR 9000, GSR 12000 Routers

Table 1-4 Cisco Campus Hardware Platform Support

IOS Platform	Switching Hardware Platform
IOS	3500, 3750, 4900, 6500 Catalyst Switches
IOS	1600, 1700, 1850, 2600, 2700, 3500, 3600, 3700 Wireless AP
IOS-XE	3650, 3850, 4500 Series Catalyst Switches
IOS-XE	5760 Wireless LAN Controller
NX-OS	3000, 5500, 6000 and 7000 Nexus Switches

Naming Conventions

There are unique filename formats for each IOS platform type. The primary IOS platforms include standard IOS, IOS-XE, IOS-XR and NX-OS software. The naming conventions are designed to convey hardware platform, feature set support, version, run code and file type. The standard IOS and IOS-XE filename conventions are discussed here.

Cisco IOS Filename Format

The IOS filename structure varies somewhat with IOS software platform. The standard components are explained with the following descriptions.

- **Hardware Platform:** Denoted with the IOS image such as c3750e, c2900 and cat3k_ caa for example.

- **Feature Set License:** Included with the IOS image file. The available feature set packages vary with hardware product line. The Cisco access switches share a common feature set architecture. In addition the ISR series routers support specific feature set packages. The Catalyst access switches are based on a Universal image that includes all feature set packages for the release version. That would include LAN Base, IP Base and IP Services for Catalyst access switches. Note that Cisco is migrating toward a single Universal package for each product line. There is IP Base that is still available as a separate package for 3560 and 3750 switch platforms.

- **K9 (Encryption**): Supports encryption protocols such as SSH and IPsec with the IOS image file. That is available for export as well to countries where permitted.

- **No Payload Encryption (NPE):** The NPE version of the IOS image file does not include encryption features. The NPE image is designed for export to countries where there are import restrictions on encryption features. The NPE files do not include MAC Sec (802.1ae) MAC security encryption feature for .bin and .tar file types. The file designator is noted as Non MAC Sec to verify it is suitable for export to countries where it isn't permitted.

- **Memory Run Code:** Applies only to the .bin file type and describe where the file is run from. The supported location for Catalyst access switches is currently from DRAM system memory only. There are additional memory run codes available with the ISR router platform including the following. F =Flash, M=DRAM, R=ROM, L=Relocatable

- **Compressed** file designator (z) applies only to .bin files

- **Version Number** includes the mainline release, train identifier, maintenance number and rebuild number where applicable. The release status (i.e early deployment) is specified on the Cisco file download page and not with the IOS filename.

- **File type** is either the .bin and .tar files. The .tar file includes the web-based device manager interface for configuring devices.

Catalyst Switch IOS Image Filenames

The standard IOS software is designed to run on most Catalyst switches, ISR routers and wireless access points. That includes Cisco IOS 12.x and IOS 15.x release software. The IOS files are based on release version and feature set. The files available vary with the hardware platform and product line. For instance some older Catalyst switch platforms provide bin and tar files for IP Services and Express setup files. The following is a list of IOS image files available. The memory requirements lists the first number as DRAM memory and the second as Flash memory

2960X Series Switches

Universal
c2960x-universalk9-mz.150-2a.EX5.bin   128 MB / 64 MB

Universal w/ Device Manager
c2960x-universalk9-tar.150-2a.EX5.tar   128 MB / 64 MB

3560X Series Switches

IP Base
c3560e-ipbasek9-mz.150-2.SE8.bin   128 MB / 64 MB

IP Base w/ Device Manager
c3560e-ipbasek9-tar.150-2.SE8.tar   128 MB / 64 MB

IP Base No Mac Sec
c3560e-ipbasek9npe-mz.150-2.SE8.bin   128 MB / 64 MB

IP Base No Mac Sec w/ Device Manager
c3560e-ipbasek9npe-tar.150-2.SE8.tar   128 MB / 64 MB

Universal
c3560e-universalk9-mz.150-2.SE8.bin   128 MB / 64 MB

Universal w/ Device Manager
c3560e-universalk9-tar.150-2.SE8.tar   128 MB / 64 MB

Universal No Mac Sec
c3560e-universalk9npe-mz.150-2.SE8.bin   128 MB / 64 MB

Universal No Mac Sec w/ Device Manager
c3560e-universalk9npe-tar.150-2.SE8.tar   128 MB / 64 MB

3750X Series Switches

Universal
c3750e-ipbasek9-mz.150-2.SE8.bin   256 MB / 64 MB

Universal w/Device Manager
c3750e-ipbasek9-tar.150-2.SE8.tar   256 MB / 64 MB

IP Base w/ Non MAC Sec
c3750e-ipbasek9npe-mz.150-2.SE8.bin   256 MB / 64 MB

IP Base w/ Non MAC Sec and Device Mgr.
c3750e-ipbasek9npe-tar.150-2.SE8.tar   256 MB / 64 MB

Universal
c3750e-universalk9-mz.150-2.SE8.bin   256 MB / 64 MB

Universal w/ Device Manager
c3750e-universalk9-tar.150-2.SE8.tar   256 MB / 64 MB

Universal w/Non MAC Sec
c3750e-universalk9npe-mz.150-2.SE8.bin   256 MB / 64 MB

Universal w/Non MAC Sec and Device Mgr.
c3750e-universalk9npe-tar.150-2.SE8.tar   256 MB / 64 MB

3750 Series Switch Filename Examples

The following are filename examples for 3750 series switches running IOS 15 release software. Catalyst 3750-X and 3750-E switches with Cisco IOS releases later than 12.2(53)SE run only the encryption supported software. Note the platform is 3750e however that file designator is shared by 3750-E and 3750-X switch platforms.

Example 1-2: Universal Bin File with Encryption Support

c3750e-universalk9-mz.152-3.E2.bin

Platform   = c3750e
Feature Set   = universalk9
M   = DRAM
Z   = compressed
Version   = 15.2(3)E2
File Type   = bin (CLI)

Example 1-3: IP Base Tar File with Encryption Support

c3750e-ipbasek9-tar.150-2.SE8.tar

Platform	= c3750e
Feature Set	= ipbasek9
Version	= 15.0(2)SE8
File Type	= tar (Device Manager)

Example 1-4: Universal Bin File with No Encryption Support

c3750e-universalk9npe-mz.150-2.SE8.bin

Platform	= c3750E
Feature Set	= universalk9npe
M	= DRAM
Z	= compressed
Version	= 15.0(2)SE8
File Type	= bin

ISR G2 Series Router Image Files

The standard IOS software is designed to run on ISR 1900, 2900 and 3900 series routers as well. The IOS files are based on release version and feature set. The files available vary with the router model. The memory requirements lists first number as DRAM and the second as Flash memory

1900 ISR G2 Series Routers

The following describes the IOS file naming convention for ISR 1921, 1941, and 1941W series routers.

Universal
c1900-universalk9-mz.SPA.153-3.M6.bin   512 MB / 256 MB

Universal-No Payload Encryption
c1900-universalk9_npe-mz.SPA.153-3.M6.bin   512 MB / 256 MB

2900 ISR G2 Series Routers

The following describes the IOS file naming convention for ISR 2901, 2911, 2921, and 2951 series routers.

Universal (2951)
C2951-universalk9-mz.SPA.153-3.M6.bin   512 MB / 256 MB

Universal-No Payload Encryption (2951)
C2951-universalk9_npe-mz.SPA.153-3.M6.bin   512 MB / 256 MB

Universal
C2900-universalk9-mz.SPA.153-3.M6.bin   512 MB / 256 MB

Universal-No Payload Encryption
C2900-universalk9_npe-mz.SPA.153-3.M6.bin   512 MB / 256 MB

3900 ISR G2 Series Routers

The following describes the IOS file naming convention for ISR 3925, 3925E, 3945 and 3945E series routers.

Universal (3925/3945)
c3900-universalk9-mz.SPA.153-3.M6.bin   1024 MB / 256 MB

Universal-No Payload Encryption (3925/3945)
c3900-universalk9_npe-mz.SPA.153-3.M6.bin   1024 MB / 256 MB

Universal (3925E / 3945E)
c3900e-universalk9-mz.SPA.153-3.M6.bin   1024 MB / 256 MB

Universal-No Payload Encryption (3925E/3945E)
c3900e-universalk9_npe-mz.SPA.153-3.M6.bin   1024 MB / 256 MB

ISR G2 Series Router Filename Examples

The following filename examples are for 3900 and 2900 series router models. The hardware platform designator for the 2951 router is c2951. The ISR G2 router models are running IOS 15.x release software.

Example 1-5 3925/3945 Universal Image Bin File w/ Encryption

    c3900-universalk9-mz.SPA.153-3.M6.bin

Platform	= c3900 (3925/3945)
Feature Set	= universalk9 (encryption support)
M	= DRAM
Z	= compressed
Digital Signature	= SPA
Version	= 15.3(3) M6 (MD)
File Type	= bin (CLI)

Example 1-6 Cisco 2921 Universal Image No Encryption

c3900e-universalk9_npe-mz.SPA.153-3.M6.bin

Platform	= c2900 (2901/2911/2921)
Feature Set	= universal_npe
M	= DRAM
Z	= compressed
Digital Signature	= SPA
Version	= 15.3(3) M6 (MD)
File Type	= bin (CLI)

802.11n Access Point Image Files

Cisco 802.11n wireless access points run standard IOS software. The 802.11n platforms provide Autonomous and Lightweight Access Point Protocol (LWAPP) architecture with indoor and outdoor IOS image files.

Table 1-5 Cisco 802.11n Indoor Access Point IOS Image Filenames

Platform	Architecture	Filename	DRAM/Flash
1600i	Autonomous	ap1g2-k9w7-tar.153-3.JBB2.tar	256 MB / 32 MB
1600i	LWAPP	ap1g2-k9w8-tar.153-3.JBB2.tar	256 MB / 32 MB
1700i	Autonomous	ap3g2-k9w7-tar.153-3.JBB2.tar	512 MB / 64 MB
1700i	LWAPP	ap3g2-k9w8-tar.153-3.JBB2.tar	512 MB / 64 MB
1850i	LWAPP	ap1g4-k9w8-tar.153-3.JBB2.tar	128 MB / 128 MB
2600i	IOS Boot	ap3g2-boot-m.124-25e.JA1.bin	64 MB / 32 MB
2600i	Autonomous	ap3g2-k9w7-tar.153-3.JBB2.tar	256 MB / 32 MB
2600i	LWAPP	ap3g2-k9w8-tar.153-3.JBB2.tar	256 MB / 32 MB
2700i	Autonomous	ap3g2-k9w7-tar.153-3.JBB2.tar	512 MB / 64 MB
2700i	LWAPP	ap3g2-k9w8-tar.153-3.JBB2.tar	512 MB / 64 MB
3500i	Autonomous	ap3g1-k9w7-tar.153-3.JBB2.tar	128 MB / 32 MB
3500i	LWAPP	ap3g1-k9w8-tar.153-3.JBB2.tar	128 MB / 32 MB
3600i	Autonomous	ap3g2-k9w7-tar.153-3.JBB2.tar	256 MB / 32 MB
3600i	LWAPP	ap3g2-k9w8-tar.153-3.JBB2.tar	256 MB / 32 MB
3700i	Autonomous	ap3g2-k9w7-tar.153-3.JBB2.tar	512 MB / 64 MB
3700i	LWAPP	ap3g2-k9w8-tar.153-3.JBB2.tar	512 MB / 64 MB

There is a separate file format for each hardware platform. The Wireless LAN Controller (WLC) software runs proprietary software for that hardware platform. The memory requirements lists the first number as DRAM memory and the second as Flash memory. The following describes the IOS file naming convention for the Cisco 1600 series autonomous access point.

Example 1-7 Cisco 1600 Series Indoor Autonomous Access Point

ap1g2-k9w7-tar.153-3.JBB2.tar

Platform	= ap1g2 (1600 Series)
Feature Set	= k9 (encryption support)
Architecture	= w7 (autonomous)
File Type	= tar (device manager)
Release Version	= 15.3(3) JBB2(ED)

Cisco Catalyst IOS-XE Image Files

The following describes the IOS-XE naming convention for Catalyst 3650 and 3850 series switches. There is a separate file format for the ASR 1000 routers. The 3650 and 3850 series switches provide only two IOS image to select from as part of IOS software selection. The memory requirements lists the first number as DRAM and the second as Flash memory.

Universal (512 MB / 245.71 MB)
cat3k_caa-universalk9.SPA.03.03.05.SE.150-1.EZ5.bin

Universal w/o DTLS (245.71 MB Flash)
cat3k_caa-universalk9ldpe.SPA.03.03.05.SE.150-1.EZ5.bin

Example 1-8: Cisco Catalyst 3850 Series Switches

cat3k_caa-universalk9.SPA.03.07.00.E.152-3.E.bin

Platform Name	= cat3k_caa
Bundle Feature Set	= universalk9
Digital Signed Version	= SPA
IOS XE release version	= 3.7.0SE
IOS image version	= 15.2(3)E
File Type	= bin

IOS Release Version

The software platforms include Standard IOS, IOS-XE, IOS-XR and NX-OS. The naming conventions for the releases versions vary with IOS software platform and code level. The code levels currently available for standard IOS include IOS 12 and IOS 15 releases. The standard Cisco IOS Software releases use a format with five components to denote release version. The format describes the naming convention that convey release version, maintenance rebuild and bug fixes.

Cisco IOS Software Releases

The IOS 12 software releases are comprised of mainline and train versions. The train version includes additional bug fixes and support for new features and hardware. The train releases are eventually integrated into subsequent mainline releases. In addition multiple maintenance releases exist for bug fixes. The maintenance release is a separate IOS release for mainline and train versions. The number is noted with the brackets and bug fixes with subsequent release are cumulative.

Release Version = A.B(C)D [E]

A.B = Major Release Number

C = Maintenance Version Number. There are additional bug fixes with each new maintenance version. The maintenance versions are cumulative where subsequent versions include new features, bug fixes and hardware support.

D = Train Identifier (Minor Release), that is an extension of a major release. The train updates provide new features and hardware support.

E = Release status based on IOS 12.0 or IOS 15.0 life cycle

Example 1-9: 3750 Series Switch IOS 12.2 Mainline Train (MD)

12.2(55)SE9 (MD)

12 = major release
2 = minor release
55 = maintenance version
SE = technology train identifier
9 = train rebuild number
MD = maintenance deployment

29

Example 1-10: 3750 Series Switch IOS 12.2 SE

    12.2(55)SE10 (ED)

    12 = major release
     2 = minor release
    55 = maintenance version
    SE = technology train identifier
    10 = train rebuild number
    ED = early deployment

Example 1-11: 3900 ISR G2 Router IOS 15.3

    15.3(3)M6 (MD)

    15 = major release
     3 = minor release
     3 = feature release
    M = maintenance release
     6 = rebuild number
    MD = maintenance deployment

Example 1-12: 3900 ISR G2 Router IOS 15.5

    15.5(2)T1 (ED)

    15 = major release
     5 = minor release
     2 = feature release
    T = technology train
     1 = rebuild number
    ED = early deployment

Example 1-13: 3850 Series Switch IOS-XE

    3.3(5)SE (ED)

    3 = major release
    3 = feature release
    5 = maintenance release rebuild number
    SE = technology train release
    ED = early deployment

Table 1-6 IOS, IOS-XE and NX-OS Software Summary

IOS Release	IOS Trains	Description
15	15M and 15T	Adds new software features and hardware to Cisco IOS Software 12.4T train. Unlike 12.4 and 12.4T, Cisco IOS Software 15 releases are a single train with extended and standard maintenance releases.
12.4	12.4 Mainline	Adds new software features and hardware support to Cisco IOS Software 12.3T train and additional software fixes.
	12.4T	Provides Cisco IOS software features and hardware support for new technology not available in the Cisco IOS Software 12.4 mainline train.
	12.4 SD and ED	Cisco IOS software features and hardware support for the market introduction of new platforms.
	12.4J and 15.2JB	Provides Cisco IOS software support for 802.11n Wireless Access Points.
12.3	12.3 and 12.3T	The Cisco IOS software 12.3 releases are superseded by the IOS Software 12.4 release.
12.2S	12.2S	Provides Cisco IOS software feature and hardware support for service provider platforms.
	12.2SB	Provides Cisco IOS software feature and hardware support for broadband and leased-line and (MPLS) service provider network.
	12.2SE	Cisco IOS software feature and hardware support for Ethernet LAN switching Cisco Catalyst 2960, 3560 and 3750 Switches.
	12.2SG	Cisco IOS software feature and hardware support for the Cisco Catalyst 4500 Series Supervisor Engine Supervisor Engine and 4900 switches.
	12.2SR	Cisco IOS software features and hardware support for service providers with Metro Ethernet, MPLS
	12.2SX	Cisco IOS software feature and hardware support for Ethernet data center switching platforms.
IOS XE	3.2, 3.3, 3.6, 3.7	Cisco IOS XE software supports the Catalyst 3650 and 3850 series access switches. The switches are next generation access switches. IOS-XE supports the Catalyst 4500E Supervisor Engines as well.
IOS XE	3.10 - 3.16	Cisco IOS XE software supports the Cisco ASR 1000 Series internet edge routers. There is new in-service software upgrades and software redundancy available.
NX-OS	6.0, 6.1, 6.2, 7.0	Cisco NX-OS software is a data-center-class operating system for the Nexus switch platform. That includes 3000, 5000, 6000, 7000 and 9000 series switches.

Table 1-7 Hardware Platform and Primary IOS Trains

Hardware Platform	Primary Train
1900, 2900, and 3900 ISR Router	IOS 15.1M
ASR 1000 Series Routers	IOS XE 3.9 IOS XE 3.8
10000 Series Routers	IOS 12.2SB
ASR 9000 Series Routers	IOS XR 3.9 IOS XR 3.8 IOS XR 3.7
12000 Series Routers	IOS 12.0S IOS 12.0SY
Nexus 9000 Switch	NX-OS 6.1
Nexus 7000 Switch	NX-OS 6.2
Nexus 5000 Switch	NX-OS 5.2
Nexus 4000 Switch	NX-OS 4.1E
Nexus 3000 Switch	NX-OS 6.0.2A
Nexus 1000V Switch	NX-OS 4.0SV
Catalyst 2960, 2970, 3560, and 3750 Series Switches	IOS 12.2SE
Catalyst 3560E, 3560X, 3750E, and 3750X Series Switches	IOS 15.2E
Catalyst 3650 and 3850 Series Switches	IOS 3.3SE
Catalyst 4500 and 4900 Series Switches	IOS 12.2SG
Catalyst 4500E and 4500-X Series Switches	IOS 3.5E
Catalyst 6500 Series Switches	IOS 12.2SX IOS 15.1SY
Wireless LAN controller 5760	IOS XE 3.3.0
3600, 3500, 2600, 1600, 1550, 1530, 1260, 1140, 1040 Access Points	IOS 15.2JB IOS 12.4J

Cisco Switch and Router Platforms

The following provide specific hardware profiles for the most common network device platforms. That would include Cisco access switches, WAN routers and Nexus data center switches.

Cisco Catalyst Access Switches

The most popular switches being deployed today for desktop connectivity include the Cisco 3750 and 3560 series switches. The 3750 and 3560 network switches are used for desktop connectivity and deployed in the wiring closet. The fixed module switches don't use a Supervisor Engine and often have power supply redundancy as an option. The data center server farm access switch is the Cisco 4900M. It has a modular architecture with a variety of Gigabit and 10 Gigabit line cards and port counts.

Cisco Catalyst 3560-X Series Switch

- Fixed Architecture
- Access Layer (Wiring Closet)
- 24/48 x GE Port Models
- Not Stackable
- GE/10 GE Uplink Network Modules
- Redundant 1100W Power Supplies
- Switching Capacity Fabric: 160 Gbps
- Forwarding Rate: 101.2 Mpps (48 Port) / 65.5 Mpps (24 Port)

Figure 1-3 Cisco Catalyst 3560 Access Switch

Cisco Catalyst 3750-X Series Switch

- Fixed Architecture
- Access Layer (Wiring Closet)
- 24/48 x GE Port Models
- Stackable
- GE/10 GE Uplink Network Modules
- Redundant 1100W Power Supplies
- Switching Capacity Fabric: 160 Gbps
- Forwarding Rate: 101.2 Mpps (48 Port), 65.5 Mpps (24 Port)

Figure 1-4 Cisco Catalyst 3750 Access Switch

Table 1-8 Cisco 3560X-48PF-E Catalyst Switch

Feature	Description
Application	Access Layer
Switch Fabric Capacity	160 Gbps
Forwarding Rate	101.2 Mpps
Redundancy	Power Supply
Architecture	Fixed
Switch Ports	48
Memory	256 MB DRAM, 64 MB Flash
Uplinks	Upgrade
Module Upgrades	4 x 1 GE (SFP), 2 x 10 GE (SFP), 2 x 10GB-T
Power Supply	1100W
PoE Support	Yes
MAC Addresses	3,000
Active VLANs	1,005

Table 1-9 Cisco 3750X-48PF-E Catalyst Switch

Feature	Description
Application	Access Layer
Switch Fabric Capacity	160 Gbps
Forwarding Rate	101.2 Mpps
Redundancy	Link, Power Supply, StackPower
Architecture	Fixed
Switch Ports	48
Memory	256 MB DRAM, 64 MB Flash
Uplinks	Upgrade
Module Upgrades	4 x 1 GE (SFP), 2 x 10 GE (SFP), 2 x 10GB-T
Power Supply	1100W
PoE Support	Yes
MAC Addresses	3,000
Active VLANs	1,005

Cisco Catalyst 3850 Series Switch

The Catalyst 3850 is the next generation 3K series switch platform for the enterprise network. It is based on the newer IOS-XE code that separates the data and control plane for a modular software architecture. There is support for faster uplinks and 480 Gbps throughput across the stack. In addition there is integrated WLC to manage access points and easy RTU licensing model. The Catalyst 3850 switch supports the new Cisco programmable ASIC called the Unified Access Data Plane (UADP). The ASIC converge processing of wired and wireless traffic to a single data plane and enable SDN cloud based services.

Fixed Architecture

- Access Layer (Wiring Closet)
- 12/16/24/48 x GE Uplink Ports
- Integrated Wireless LAN Controller
- Stackable
- 1/10/40 GE Uplink Network Modules
- Redundant 1100W Power Supplies
- Stack Throughput: 480 Gbps
- Forwarding Rate: 130.95 Mpps (48 Port), 500 Mpps (24 Port)

Table 1-10 Cisco Catalyst 3850 Series Switch

Feature	Description
Application	Access Layer
Switch Fabric Capacity	640 Gbps
Max. Forwarding Rate	480 Mpps
Redundancy	Uplink, Power Supply, StackPower
Architecture	Fixed
Switch Ports	12/16/24/48 Ports
Memory	4 GB/8 GB DRAM / 2 GB, 4 GB, 8 GB Flash
Uplinks	Upgrade
Module Upgrades	4 x 1 GE (SFP), 4 x 10 GE (SFP), 8 x 10 GE (SFP+), 2 x 40 GB (QSFP+)
Power Supply	1100W
PoE Support	Yes
MAC Addresses	32,000
Active VLANs	4,000
Access Points	100
Wireless Clients	2000

Cisco Catalyst 4510R+E Switch

The Cisco 4500 switch is typically deployed as a distribution layer switch at larger branch offices and smaller data centers. There are multiple Supervisor Engines and line cards available with the 4500 series switches. The line cards are a mix of various GE and 10 GE switch interfaces. The Supervisor Engine and line card support is chassis specific. The Catalyst 4500 Supervisor Engine performance throughput varies according to model. The VSS switch feature is now supported as well. The following describe standard features available with the Catalyst 4510R+E distribution switch.

- Modular Architecture
- Distribution Layer
- 10 Chassis Slots
- 384 x GE Ports
- 104 x 10 GE Ports
- Redundant Supervisor Engines
- Supervisor Engine Support: V-10GE, 6E, 7E
- 9000W Redundant Power Supplies
- Switching Capacity: 848 Gbps (7E)
- Forwarding Rate: 250 Mpps (7E)

Figure 1-5 Cisco Catalyst 4510R+E Switch

Cisco Catalyst 6500E Distribution Switch

The newer Cisco 6500E (enhanced chassis) includes faster Supervisor Engine support. There are four 6500E series switch chassis available including the 6503E, 6506E, 6509E and 6513E. Each chassis has a specific number of slots available. The Supervisor Engine (processor) hardware will determine the minimum IOS version required.

- Modular Architecture
- Distribution/Core Layer
- 13 Slot Chassis
- 576 x GE Ports
- 176 x 10 GE Ports
- 44 x 40 GE Ports
- Redundant Supervisor Engines
- Supervisor Engine Support: 32, 720, VS-S720, VS-S2T
- Multiple Service Modules
- Redundant 8700W Power Supplies
- Chassis Switching Capacity: 4 Tbps (VS-S2T)
- Chassis Forwarding Rate: 720 Mpps (VS-S2T)

Figure 1-6 Cisco Catalyst 6513E Switch

Cisco ISR G2 Series Routers

Cisco 2900 ISR G2

The Cisco 2900 G2 series ISR router is a branch router with a modular architecture designed for scalability and performance. There is protocol support for a variety of LAN/WAN interfaces and enhancements for voice, video, data and wireless traffic. The three models include the Cisco 2901, 2911, 2921 and 2951 routers. There are a variety of integrated features including Unified Communications Manager, support for virtualization, WAAS, Wireless LAN Controllers and Video services.

Cisco 3900 ISR G2

The Cisco 3900 ISR router is a distribution and core office router with a modular style architecture designed for scalability and performance. There is protocol support for a variety of LAN/WAN interfaces and enhancements for voice, video, data and wireless traffic. The four models include the Cisco 3925 and 3925E, 3945 and 3945E routers. The E-series have increased throughput and additional scalability with the same services of the ISR platform. Table 1-11 lists router performance for the 2900 and 3900 series ISR G2 routers using various packet sizes with QoS, ACL and NAT services enabled. The router WAN throughput capacity of the 3945E is a maximum 350 Mbps with concurrent network services.

Figure 1-7 Cisco 3945E ISR G2 Router

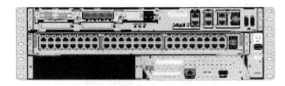

Cisco 3900 ISR G2 Processor

The Cisco 3900 ISR routers use integrated multi-core processors that are not upgradeable (fixed module architecture). The service modules and WAN interface cards forward packets across the backplane fabric to other service modules at 2 Gbps. As with the Cisco 6500 switch, the routing table is managed by the route processor. The CEF system tables (including FIB and adjacency table) are derived from the routing table.

Cisco 3900 ISR G2 Etherswitch

The Cisco Enhanced Etherswitch service modules support CEF Layer 2 and Layer 3 switching in hardware. The result is performance throughput is increased significantly. Note that hardware switching is not supported by all Ethernet modules. Any forwarding of packets toward the route processor for Layer 3 processing such as routing table updates is at 4 Gbps. In addition to Cisco Express Forwarding (CEF), integrating the Ethernet switch module with the router improves network performance. Instead of switch uplinks, all packets are switched across the high speed Multi Gigabit Fabric (MGF). Note as well that only service modules designed for the MGF can forward packets across that fabric. Any modules not fabric enabled use the PCI Express link.

Table 1-11 Cisco 2900 and 3900 Series ISR G2 Router Capacity

Model	CEF Forwarding	WAN Throughput
3945E ISR G2	982,000 pps	350 Mbps
3925E ISR G2	833,000 pps	250 Mbps
2951 ISR G2	580,000 pps	75 Mbps
2921 ISR G2	480,000 pps	50 Mbps
2911 ISR G2	353,000 pps	35 Mbps
2901 ISR G2	327,000 pps	25 Mbps

WAN Throughput

- 3945 ISR G2 = 150 Mbps
- 3925 ISR G2 = 100 Mbps
- 3925E is the 3925 with an upgrade from SPE-100 to SPE-200
- 3945E is the 3945 with an upgrade from SPE-150 to SPE-250

Service Modules

The Cisco 3900 G2 Integrated Services Router (ISR) uses a service module slot for LAN (campus) interfaces. The performance is optimized with 4 Gbps connectivity to the route processor and 2 Gbps switching capacity across the Multi-Gigabit System Fabric (MGF) to other service modules. This technology replaces the older network modules and enhanced network and voice modules. The result is higher port density support and increased power support enabling faster interfaces and scalability.

The Etherswitch service module is used for campus connectivity and includes Fast Ethernet (100 Mbps) and Gigabit (1000 Mbps). The 16 port Fast Ethernet module is comprised of 15 Fast Ethernet ports and 1 Gigabit port. The 24 port module is comprised of 23 Fast Ethernet ports and 1 Gigabit port. There is a 48 port Fast Ethernet and 16, 24 and 48 port Gigabit Ethernet modules. The WAN interface cards include high speed voice and WAN for Serial T1, E1, T3, E3, DSL and Gigabit Metro Ethernet connectivity. The Cisco 3900 Services Ready Engine (SRE) slot provides for fast deployment of network services including WAAS, Cisco Unity Express, Wireless LAN Controllers (WLC) and network applications. The SRE has an onboard multi-core processor and 1 TB of disk storage.

Cisco 3900 ISR G2 Memory

The same types of memory are used for both switch and router platforms. That includes Flash, NVRAM and DRAM. Each router model has default and upgrade memory options to enhance router performance. Routers as with all networking equipment, perform best when memory is maximized. The following is a description of typical memory deployed with the Cisco 3900 ISR G2. Note that each router platform include onboard DRAM memory.

Dynamic RAM (DRAM)

This is the system memory used by the route processor. It comprises most of the memory deployed at routers. The purpose of DRAM is to load and run the Cisco IOS system software, routing table, CEF system tables and the configuration file. The Cisco 3900 ISR G2 router is deployed with a default of 1 GB DRAM and 4 GB maximum upgrade.

External Compact Flash

The main purpose of Flash Memory is to store the router IOS system image file. The default Flash Memory is 256 MB with 8 GB maximum upgrade.

NVRAM

This memory type is very fast and primarily used for storing the startup configuration script. Both switches and routers use NVRAM for this purpose. There is a default of 256 KB memory onboard the 3900 ISR G2 router.

Table 1-12 Cisco 2911, 2921 and 2951 ISR G2 Routers

Feature	2911 ISR	2921 ISR	2951 ISR
Application	Branch Office	Branch Office	Branch Office
Throughput	35 Mbps	50 Mbps	75 Mbps
Redundancy	Power Supply	Power Supply	Power Supply
Architecture	Modular	Modular	Modular
ESM Ports	24 GE, 48 GE	24 GE, 48 GE	24 GE, 48 GE
Uplinks	3 x GE	3 x GE	3 x GE
Module Upgrades	Service Module(1) EHWIC(4), ISM(1) PVDM3(2) Compact Flash SRE, WAAS	Service Module(1) EHWIC(4), ISM(1) PVDM3(3) Compact Flash SRE, WAAS	Service Module(2) EHWIC(4), ISM(1) PVDM3(3) Compact Flash SRE, WAAS
Power Supply	200W	280W	370W

Table 1-13 Cisco 3925 and 3945 ISR G2 Routers

Feature	3925	3945
Application	Distribution	Distribution/Core Office
Throughput	100 Mbps	150 Mbps
Redundancy	Power Supply, S.M	Power Supply, S.M
Architecture	Modular	Modular
ESM Switch Ports	74 GE, 98 GE	74 GE, 98 GE
Switch Uplinks	3 x GE	3 x GE
Module Upgrades	Service Module (2), EHWIC(4), PVDM3(4), ISM(1), Compact Flash, SRE, SPE(100), WAAS	Service Module (4), EHWIC(4), PVDM3(4), ISM(1), Compact Flash, SRE, SPE(150), WAAS
Power Supply	520W	520W

Table 1-14 Cisco 3925E and 3945E ISR G2 Routers

Feature	3925E	3945E
Application	Core Office	Core Office/Internet
Throughput	250 Mbps	350 Mbps
Redundancy	Power Supply, Module	Power Supply, Module
Architecture	Modular	Modular
ESM Switch Ports	74 GE, 98 GE	74 GE, 98 GE
Switch Uplinks	4 x GE	4 x GE
Module Upgrades	Service Module (2), EHWIC(3), PVDM3(3), Compact Flash, SRE, SPE(200), WAAS	Service Module (4), EHWIC(3), PVDM3(3), Compact Flash, SRE, SPE(250), WAAS
Power Supply	520W	520W

Chapter 2

Managing IOS Software

Selecting IOS Software

The hardware platforms will require selection of networking software. It is a key component of any effective network design. The hardware platform and feature set requirements is the basis of IOS selection. The network engineer would select from multiple IOS versions and feature sets bundled with a .bin or .tar file for download.

The hardware platforms for the campus design is comprised of switches, wireless devices and server load balancers. In addition the WAN design is comprised of routers and WAAS optimizers. Figure 2-1 is the recommended strategy and sequence for selecting IOS software.

Figure 2-1 Strategy for Selecting IOS Software

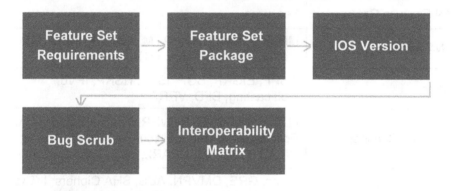

Feature Set Requirements

The feature set requirements is comprised of various networking, security and management features. It is used as the basis for selecting networking software. The feature support enables connectivity to multiple WAN endpoints. That is required for integrating the enterprise with branch offices, partners, mobile employees and customers.

The feature set requirements is comprised of various networking, security and management features. It is used as the basis for selecting networking software. The campus feature set support enables connectivity of campus devices and network servers. That is required for integrating the data center with the WAN infrastructure and access to applications. The branch offices, partners, mobile employees and customers connect across the WAN to the enterprise data center. The following is a list of top level feature set groups for campus devices.

WAN Routers

The primary features available with WAN/Internet routers are based on routing and WAN protocols. The equipment and software must support common dynamic routing protocols and features. In addition there are branch office and data center WAN services. Optimized security has been developed for routers recently with the proliferation of security attacks.

As mentioned performance problems including network latency and throughput occur across the WAN. Application services are supported for optimizing application traffic. The following describes standard feature set requirements for WAN routers. The features are distributed across all feature set packages for routers.

Table 1-15 Typical WAN Router Networking Features

WAN Feature Groups	Features
WAN Protocols	MPLS, Frame Relay, ATM, SONET, Serial, DSL, Metro Ethernet, Cable, OTV, LISP
Routing	OSPF, EIGRP, BGP, IS-IS, HSRP, IPV6, Multicasting, BFD, VRRP
Application Services	LLQ, CBWFQ, SRR, WRR, Traffic Shaping, CAR, Policing, Performance Routing, Akamai Connect, WAAS, WCCPv2, NBAR2, AVC, Load Balancing
Security	IPsec, GRE, DMVPN, AES, SHA Ciphers, IKEv2, ACL, PVLAN, 802.1X, NAC, SSL, TACACS, RADIUS, DHCP Snooping, Dynamic ARP Inspection, IP Source Guard, VACL, RACL, PACL, CWS, IPS, IOS SSL, Firewall Zones, AAA
Management	SNMP v2, v3, SSH, IP SLA, NetFlow, Syslog, SPAN, EEM, NTP
IP Telephony	MGCP, SIP, H.323, SCCP, SRST, Toll-Bypass, SRSV, SRTP, TLS, IVR, DTMF, SFTP

WAAS Optimization Platform

The following is a typical feature set for the Cisco WAAS platform. The WAAS platforms have four feature set packages. The WAAS platforms include physical, module, IOS and virtual solutions. The supported features are based on the WAAS platform and feature set package.

- TFO - Scaling, SACK, Local ACK, BIC, Initial Congestion Window
- Application Acceleration - HTTP, HTTPS, CIFS, MAPI, Citrix, NFS
- Protocol Acceleration – Read-Ahead, Connection Reuse, Pipelining
- Data Redundancy Elimination (DRE)
- LZ Compression
- WCCPv2 Interception
- AppNav
- Akamai Connect
- Video Optimizer
- Virtualization
- NetFlow v9

Global Server Load Balancer (GSLB)

The following include the standard feature set for global server load balancer. It is based on various DNS services and protocol support. Edge device redundancy for global load balancers is supported with VRRP. That allows the network engineer to deploy device redundancy with the WAN design. The redundancy modes for most networking devices include active/active and active/standby. The active/active mode enables packet forwarding from both load balancers simultaneously.

- Network protocols
- Load balancing algorithms
- VRRP (Redundancy)
- SSL acceleration
- DNSSEC
- DNS cache
- DNS firewall
- IP Anycast
- IPv6 support
- Server health monitoring
- Network Address Translation (NAT)

Campus Switches

The Cisco feature set groups for a hardware platform is often distributed across multiple feature set packages. There are often licenses for additional security application services and telephony. The design requirements would determine what packages are required. The following list comprises a typical feature set for access and multilayer campus switches.

Table 1-16 Campus Switch Networking Feature Set

Feature Set Group	Features
Switching	RPVST+, MST, UDLD, LACP, 802.1q, PagP, VTP, Jumbo Frames, Dynamic VLAN, FabricPath, OTV, 802.3ae, 802.3z, MEC, PoE, VDC, FEX
Routing	OSPF, EIGRP, HSRP, IPV6, Multicasting, BFD, NSF/SSO
Application Services	SSR, WRR, CBWFQ, Policing, AVC, Load Balancing
Security	ACL, Port Security, PVLAN, 802.1x, NAC, TACACS, RADIUS, DHCP Snooping, Dynamic ARP Inspection, IP Source Guard, VACL, RACL, PACL, IPS, AAA
Management	SNMP v2, v3, SSH, NetFlow, Syslog, SPAN, EEM, NTP
IP Telephony	Voice VLAN, AutoQoS

Cisco Wireless Devices

There are various new performance and security enhancement features available with Cisco wireless network services. The standard and newer wireless features include WPA2, AES Encryption, EAP, IPS, MIMO, QoS, Channel Bonding and RRM.

Campus Server Load Balancer

The following list comprises a typical feature set for campus load balancers. There are campus load balancers available from multiple vendors. Each vendor provides a feature set based on their licensing model.

Table 1-17 Campus Server Load Balancer Feature Set

Load Balancing	Networking	Security	Optimization
• Network Protocols • L4 Algorithms • Content Switching • RTMP/RTSP streaming	• DNS Proxy • IPv6 • Routing Protocols • LACP • 802.1q • NAT • VRRP	• AAA • ADS • LDAP • SAML • DNS Firewall	• SSL Acceleration • Caching • Compression • TCP Optimization • Adaptive Rate Control • AppFlow

Cisco Feature Navigator

The Navigator is available to research features and obtain recommended feature set and IOS release version for a hardware platform. The memory and flash requirements are listed for each IOS image as well. The selection is based on hardware platform and feature set requirements. Research and compare to select optimal IOS version and licensing for the hardware.

Figure 2-2 Cisco Feature Navigator

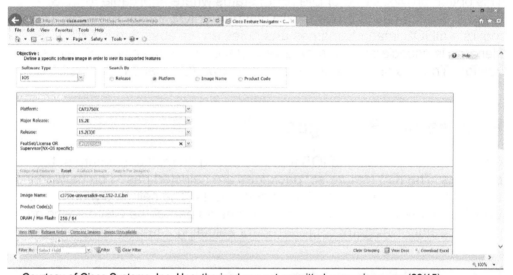

Courtesy of Cisco Systems, Inc. Unauthorized use not permitted, www.cisco.com (09/15)

Research Software

This option provides feature information for a specific IOS release version. The tool lists all supported features for hardware running the IOS release with a feature set package. The following describe search items available

> **IOS Software Platform:** IOS, IOS-XE, IOS-XR, NX-IOS
> **Major Release:** Select from multiple mainline trains
> **Minor Release:** Select from multiple releases
> **Hardware Platform:** Select from supported hardware platforms
> **Feature Set License:** Select an available feature set package

Research Features

This option allows selection of one or more networking features and/or technologies. The Navigator provides a list of all train release IOS images that support the features/technologies selected. In addition all there is a list of all hardware platforms that support the required features or technologies.

Compare Software Releases

This option allows the network engineer to compare two IOS releases for supported features. The comparison is based on IOS platform, major release, release, hardware platform and feature set licensing. The results include IOS image, memory requirements (DRAM/Flash) and features provided for the release. There is a common feature listing as well.

IOS Image End of Life Status

This option provides End of Life (EoL) status where applicable for IOS images. Search based on hardware platform or IOS image filename. The tool lists all IOS image filenames and notes any release that is EoL. IOS filename is associated with a hardware platform and specific IOS release version. There is an option to search on known IOS filename as well.

Feature Set Packages

Cisco provides licensing of IOS features based on multiple feature set packages. The IOS feature set packages are selected based on networking, security and management feature requirements. The selected routers and WAAS optimizers support various packages as part of the Cisco licensing model. Feature Navigator is preferred for selecting a feature set package.

Cisco ISR G2 Series Routers

The following lists the IOS feature set packages available for Cisco ISR G2 routers. The IWAN Application Experience (AppX) is a feature license that supports newer optimization features for WAN routers. The Universal Image is a feature that preloads all packages and enables them with license keys.

Figure 2-3 Cisco ISR G2 Router Feature Set Packages

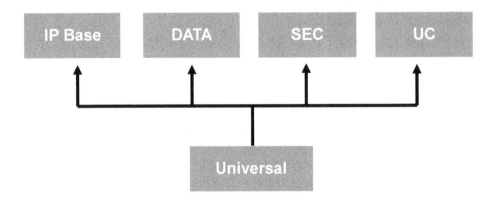

Table 1-18 Cisco ISR G2 Router Feature Set Packages

Feature Set Package	Feature Support
IP Base	Basic Switching, Routing, Security, Management
Data	MPLS, BFD, RSVP, L2VPN, L3VPN, GLBP, IP SLA, PfR, Mobile IP
Security (SEC)	IPsec, DMVPN, GRE, IKEv2, Easy VPN, GETVPN, IPS, Firewall
UCS	PSTN Gateway, H.320, H.324, Voice Conferencing, CAC, Codecs
Universal	All Features

Cisco WAAS Optimizers

The following is a description of the WAAS feature set packages available for deployment. It is a WAN optimizer deployed to the network edge.

Table 1-19 Cisco WAAS Platform Hardware Feature Set Packages

Feature Set Package	Feature Support
Transport	TFO, DRE, Compression
Enterprise	Transport license and application acceleration features for WAAS platforms. There is support for disk encryption and NetQoS as well.
Video	Supports Microsoft RTSP video stream splitting on WAVE and SRE router hardware.
Virtual Blade	Supported with WAVE appliances for hosting third party operating systems and applications.

Catalyst 2960, 3560 and 3750 Switches

The following lists the IOS feature set packages available for Cisco 2960, 3560 and 3750 access switches. The LAN Base feature set is the default shipped with new switches. The customer can order feature set upgrades as well that are pre-shipped by Cisco. The Universal Image is a newer delivery model feature that preloads all packages. They are easily enabled wit new software activation licensing. The feature set selected is based on design requirements.

Table 1-20 Cisco Catalyst 3750 Switch Feature Set Packages

Feature Set Package	Feature Support
LAN Base	Most Layer 2 Switching, SVI, No Routing, MIBs, IPSG, IP SLA Responder, RSPAN, DHCP Snooping, DAI, PACL, NAC, 802.1x, Basic QoS
IP Base	All Switching Features, HSRP, RIP, Static, EIGRP, Stack, ACL, PVLAN, TrustSec, 802.1ae, Advanced QoS, AAA
IP Services	OSPF, EIGRP, BGP, ISIS, VRF Lite, WCCP, PBR, EEM, IP SLA Initiator
Universal	All Features

Figure 2-4 Cisco Catalyst Access Switch Feature Set Packages

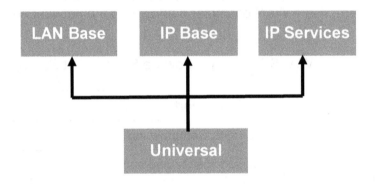

Catalyst 3850 Series Switches

The three feature sets available with Cisco Catalyst 3850 series switches include the following:

LAN Base: The default feature set offers enhanced intelligent services including standard layer 2 switching, 255 VLANs, advanced security and MQC QoS.

IP Base: Multilayer switching, 1000 VLANs, wireless controller support, routed access, smart operations, FNF, additional access point license required for mobility controller role.

IP Services: Advanced Layer 3 features with EIGRP, OSPF, BGP, PIM, IPv6, OSPFv3 and EIGRPv6.

The Cisco Catalyst 3850 Series Switches with LAN Base feature set can only stack with other Cisco Catalyst 3850 Series LAN Base switches. The same applies to IP Base and IP Services as well. A mixed stack of LAN Base switches with IP Base or IP Services is not supported. In addition the The 12-port and 24-port SFP based models can only be ordered with IP Base or IP Services licenses. Therefore, in order to stack with LAN Base models, they need to be configured in LAN Base mode from the CLI.

Catalyst 6500 Series Switches

The following describe the Catalyst 6500 Series IOS feature set packages available as of IOS 12.2(33)SXH release version.

Figure 2-5 Catalyst 6500 Series IOS Feature Set Packages

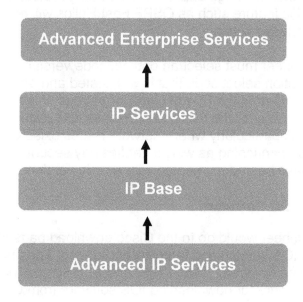

Catalyst 6500 Series Switch Feature Set Packages

The following describe the standard features available for 6500 series switches based on Cisco IOS Software package:

IP Base (Default): Basic Routing, EIGRP Stub, PIM Stub, Layer 2 Switching, Security, IPv6 Host Support and QoS.

IP Services: OSPF, EIGRP, BGP, PIM, Trustsec, CMP (2T), WCCP.

Advanced IP Services: Advanced IPv4 and IPv6, SGACLs (2T), Layer 3 VPN, MPLS, EoMPLS and VPLS.

Advanced Enterprise Services: All 6500 Cisco IOS Software Features

IOS Release Version

Cisco provides software code versions for each network device. The software code is hardware platform dependent. In addition the IOS release version enables various feature enhancements, bug fixes and security fixes. The software version selected will affect network stability, feature set support and interoperability. There are a significant number of problems that occur as a result of incorrect software code selection. The primary Cisco IOS version selector tool is called Feature Navigator.

The software code platforms available include IOS, IOS-XE, NX-OS and IOS-XR platforms. The IOS filename enables specific features from the feature set package supported. For example consider a routing design based on OSPF. That would require the IP Base feature set package for routers. The IP Base package enables most routing protocols. In addition enabling a specific feature such as OSPF Fast Hellos will require a supported IOS release version.

The network engineer must select an optimal code version with Feature Navigator. In addition select code that is well tested and approved for general release and note the End of Life (EoL) status. It is helpful as well to read the release notes for the IOS code. Discuss IOS code selection with Cisco TAC as well particularly where network issues exist. Cisco Software Checker is worth mentioning as well. It verifies any security vulnerabilities and bugs that have been documented with a code version.

Downloading IOS Software

The network engineer would go to the Cisco download page after determining the IOS version and feature set required. The primary research tools include Cisco Navigator, Cisco TAC and Bug Scrub. The following outlines the procedure for downloading IOS software from Cisco.com online.

Step 1: Select Device Type

Step 2: Select Platform Series

Step 3: Select Model Series

Step 4: Select Model / Hardware

Step 5: Select Software Type

Step 6: Select IOS Release Version

Step 7: Select IOS Image File

Step 8: Document Memory Required

Step 9: Download IOS Image

Software Download Page

The following are examples for downloading IOS software from the Cisco download page. Routers and distribution switches are complex. As a result there are separate software types based on hardware component (chassis, sup engine, interface adapter, network module etc.).

Catalyst 3750-X Access Switch

1. Select Device Type = Switches
2. Select Platform Series = Campus LAN Switches - Access
3. Select Model Series = 3750-X
4. Select Model = 3750-48-PS
5. Select Software Type = IOS Software
6. Select IOS Release Version = 15.0(1)SE8 (MD)
7. Select IOS Image File = c3750e-universalk9-mz.150-2.SE8.bin
8. Memory Requirements = 256 MB DRAM / 64 MB Flash

2921 ISR G2 Series Router

1. Select Device Type = Routers
2. Select Platform Series = Branch Routers
3. Select Model Series = 2900 Series ISR Router
4. Select Model = 2921 ISR
5. Hardware Component = Chassis Software
6. Select Software Type = IOS Software
7. Select IOS Release Version = 15.3(3)M6 (MD)
8. Select IOS Image File = c2900-universalk9-mz.SPA.153-3.M6.bin
9. Memory Requirements = 512 MB DRAM / 256 MB Flash

Catalyst 6513-E Distribution Switch

1. Select Device Type = Switches
2. Select Platform Series = Data Center Series Switches
3. Select Model Series = Data Center IOS Switches
4. Select Model = 6500 Series Switches
5. Select Chassis = 6513-E
6. Hardware Component = Supervisor Engine 2T
7. Select Software Type = IOS Software
8. Select IOS Release Version = 15.1(2)SY5 (MD)
9. Select IOS Image = s2t54-adventerprisek9-mz.SPA.151-2.SY5.bin
10. Memory Requirements = 2048 MB DRAM / 1024 MB Flash

Memory Requirements

Verify the DRAM system memory and Flash memory space available at the network device before downloading the IOS software. The show version command will lists available DRAM system memory for running the IOS image. The dir flash: command lists the available Flash memory for storing the IOS image.

> device# **show version**
> device# **dir flash:**

The DRAM and Flash memory requirements for the IOS image is shown with the IOS filename from the download page. In addition it is available from the Feature Navigator research software option. The network engineer can upgrade DRAM and/or Flash where the hardware platform supports it. In addition there is the option to delete files from Flash or select a reduced feature set with a smaller file size.

Bug Scrub Toolkit

The purpose of Cisco Bug Toolkit is to check for known bugs with the selected IOS release version. There are bugs with all software releases that are documented with Bug Toolkit. The bugs associated with the IOS release may or may not affect your network. The network design, hardware platform, features and protocols enabled would determine that. The bug scrub allows the network engineer to search Bug Toolkit based on hardware platform, IOS release or keyword search. The bug reports listed are not included in the release notes for the IOS version. That makes the bug scrub a key aspect of any IOS upgrade. In addition to the bug scrub, contact TAC support for recommended IOS code particularly when the purpose of the IOS upgrade is to fix network problems.

Cisco Interoperability Matrix

The interoperability matrix provide hardware and software guidance for networking solutions. That includes interoperability among modules deployed to a chassis and connectivity with multiple devices. Some networking features require minimum software versions across multiple infrastructure, security and management platforms. The network engineer should refer to the **software interoperability matrix** section of the release notes for requirements and recommendations. In addition Cisco will publish a hardware interoperability matrix as well for some hardware platforms.

Upgrading IOS Code

This chapter explains how to upgrade IOS code for a variety of Cisco switches and routers. The examples include bin and tar files for manual and auto upgrades. The switch upgrades are based on unstacked and stacked design configurations.

- Cisco Catalyst Series Switches (Unstacked)
- Cisco Catalyst 3750 Switch Stack
- Cisco Catalyst 3850 Switch Stack
- Cisco ISR G2 Series Routers

Cisco Catalyst Series Switches (Unstacked)

The following describes the standard IOS upgrade process for Cisco access switches. That would include the Catalyst 2960, 3560 and 3750 series switches. The 2960X switch IOS has a universal file only (with .bin and .tar with device manager). The IP services feature set is now included with the Universal image for all 3560X and 3750X switches.

IOS Upgrade (.bin)

The following procedure will upgrade the IOS image on the Cisco Catalyst series switches. It is a standard method that can be used to upgrade access and distribution series switches. Both .bin and .tar file types are included based on what is selected for download. Select from the following three methods to copy the new IOS image to switch Flash memory.

Method 1: TFTP Server

The following TFTP Server method is the most selected procedure for copying the upgraded IOS image to switch Flash memory.

Step 1: Select and download the new IOS image file from www.cisco.com

Go to www.cisco.com and download the required IOS image tar file to TFTP server. Consider the guidelines from the "Selecting IOS Software" section for optimized IOS release and feature set selection. Note the required DRAM/Flash memory required for the IOS image. Download the IOS image file to the default root directory of the TFTP server.

Step 2: Install TFTP server software (SolarWinds) to desktop.

Step 3: Connect console cable from the switch console port to desktop serial or USB interface shown with Figure 2-6.

Step 4: Connect Ethernet crossover cable from desktop Ethernet port to switch Ethernet port for IP connectivity to the switch. That is required for the actual TFTP of IOS file image to flash memory.

Figure 2-6 Desktop TFTP Connectivity to Catalyst Switch

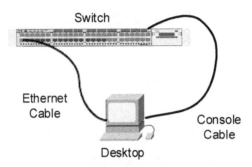

Step 5: Start PuTTY serial connection on desktop to configure the switch.

Step 6: Verify there is enough DRAM memory and Flash memory available for the selected IOS image file.

The **show version** command is used to verify the required DRAM system memory is available for the IOS image file. The **dir flash:** command verifies there is enough Flash memory available to store the image file. The required DRAM/Flash memory for the IOS file was noted from the download page.

Step 7: Configure TFTP connectivity with a VLAN interface on the switch to be in the same VLAN (subnet) as your desktop Ethernet port. The ipconfig /all command list IP settings for the desktop Ethernet NIC.

```
switch(config)# int vlan 1
switch(config-if)# ip address [ip address] [subnet mask]
switch(config-if)# no shut
switch(config-if)# exit
switch# wr mem
```

For a different subnet configure IP default-gateway command to set a default gateway to reach TFTP server.

```
switch(config)# ip default-gateway [ip address]
```

Step 8: Ping the IP address of the TFTP server from the switch. The network engineer would ping the IP address assigned to the desktop NIC. Where deployed, ping the remote TFTP server IP address. Turn off the desktop firewall temporarily if the TFTP server isn't responding.

switch# **ping** [desktop ip address]

Step 9: Copy the IOS .bin image from the TFTP directory to switch Flash.

switch# **copy tftp:** [IOS filename] **flash:**

(Optional) The following command will copy the IOS .tar file (instead of .bin) from the TFTP server with specified IP address to the remote switch flash.

switch# **archive download-sw /destination-system 1 /reload tftp://** [ip address]/c3750-universalk9-mz.122-55.SE10.tar

Method 2: USB Drive

The USB slot now available on most Cisco devices is probably the easiest option for copying IOS image to switch. The downloaded file is copied to a USB stick. The Network Engineer would copy over the file from there. Some Cisco devices only support FAT16 for USB disks. The maximum capacity USB stick (flash drive) as a result is formatted to 1 GB.

Step 1: Format the USB stick with FAT16 file system.

switch# **format usbflash0:**

Step 2: Copy the downloaded IOS image to the USB stick.

Step 3: Insert the USB stick to the switch USB port.

Step 4: Copy IOS .bin file to switch flash with the following command.

switch# **copy usbdrive0:** [IOS filename] **flash:**

(Optional) The following command will copy the IOS .tar file (instead of .bin) from USB Flash drive to switch Flash memory:

switch# **archive download-sw / /reload usbflash0://IOS_filename.tar**

Method 3: Telnet

The Telnet session provides remote connectivity to the network switch for IOS upgrade. The network switch must already be configured with an IP address advertised on the network. The example includes the commands for downloading the .bin file or .tar file. The .tar file option includes Device Manager to manage switches from a web browser.

Step 1: Install TFTP server software (SolarWinds) to desktop.

Step 2: Download the IOS image to the root directory of the TFTP Server.

Step 3: Start PuTTY Telnet session to switch management IP address.

Step 4: Start TFTP server software from desktop

Step 5: Copy the IOS .bin file from the TFTP server to the remote switch flash memory with the following command.

> switch# **copy tftp:** [IOS filename] **flash:**

(Optional) The following command will copy the IOS .tar file (instead of .bin) from the TFTP server with specified IP address to the remote switch flash.

switch# **archive download-sw /destination-system 1 /destination-system 2 /destination-system 3 /reload tftp://**[ip address]/c3750-universalk9-mz.122-55.SE10.tar

Step 6: Edit the switch configuration script boot marker section with new IOS image filename.

> switch# **boot system flash:** [IOS filename]
> switch# **write mem**
> switch# **show boot**
>
> BOOT path-list: flash: [filename]
> Config file: flash:/config.text
> Private Config file: flash:/private-config.text
> Enable Break: no
> Manual Boot: no
> HELPER path-list:
> Auto upgrade: yes
> Auto upgrade path:
> Timeout for Config Download: 0 seconds
> Config Download via DHCP: disabled (next boot: disabled)

Step 7: Delete old bin file (optional) after verifying all working

3750 Switch Stack IOS Upgrade

The Cisco 2960 and 3750 access switch platforms use a technique called Stacking. There are a variety of performance and availability advantages. The stack can connect a maximum grouping of up to 9 switches of the same platform with the same IOS software. The switch stack creates a unified control plane and data plane. The 3750 series switch StackWise uses a bidirectional stacking cable to connect the switches with a throughput of 32 Gbps. In addition there is StackWise Plus technology that increases backplane throughput from 32 Gbps to 64 Gbps. There is an elected master switch that manages the control plane for the stack. The switch members continue non-stop Layer 2 packet forwarding when the master switch fails.

IOS Auto-Upgrade (.TAR)

The 3750-X series switch stack members can be deployed with IP Base and IP Services feature set licenses to create a switch stack. The stack switches must have the same IOS major release version. Any switch with a different minor version number as the stack master enters version-mismatch (VM) mode and cannot join the stack with full feature support.

The master switch will upgrade (or downgrade) the new switch in VM mode with the current stack image (bin or tar file). The transparent auto-upgrade feature is available for upgrading stacked switches. Verify any switches running in VM mode with the **show switch** command. The procedure automatically copies the correct software image from any stack member tar file from the switch stack flash memory to the switch in VM mode.

The auto-upgrade option is enabled for 3750 series stacked switches when **boot auto-copy-sw** command is enabled. Verify that auto upgrade is enabled for the switch with the **show boot** command. Note the switch in VM mode must have enough Flash memory for the IOS image upgrade. For IOS downgrades verify the IOS release version supports the VM mode switch. The switch in VM mode might not run all released software. In addition earlier versions of IOS software release sometimes won't support new switch hardware features.

File Types

The software download center for switch IOS images include files with the .bin and .tar extension. The compressed .tar file includes device manager for a web-based interface to manage network devices. The following describes how to do an automatic IOS upgrade for the Cisco 3750 switch stack. The automatic upgrade applies only to .tar IOS image files. IOS images downloaded to the stack master are automatically downloaded to the connected stack members.

Summary Steps

Step 1: Select and download IOS image (.tar)
Step 2: Determine the stack master switch
Step 3: Backup the current IOS image to TFTP server
Step 4: Verify the DRAM and Flash memory available.
Step 5: Copy the IOS tar image to stack master switch
Step 6: Copy the IOS file to all stack members
Step 7: Verify boot flash variable
Step 8: Save changes, reload and verify upgrade

Step 1: Select and download the IOS image .tar file

Go to www.cisco.com and download the required IOS image tar file to TFTP server. Consider the guidelines from the "Selecting IOS Software" section for optimized IOS release and feature set selection. Note the required DRAM/Flash memory required for the IOS image.

Step 2: Determine the assigned stack master switch

The switch with the highest priority value is assigned master switch in a stack. Cisco recommends assigning priority value 15 to the switch preferred as stack master. The following example lists the priority settings for all switches as part of the stack. Switch 2 from the example is assigned as Master switch for the stack.

3750-S2# **show switch detail**

Switch#	Role	Mac Address	Priority	State
1	Slave	000a.32ae.4f00	9	Ready
*2	**Master**	000c.b2dc.1608	15	Ready

Step 3: Backup the current IOS image to TFTP server

The recommended best practice is to make a backup copy of the current IOS image to TFTP server. That allows the network engineer to restore the current IOS image if there is a problem with the upgrade. In addition having a backup allows deletion of the current IOS file to increase Flash memory where required. Include the IOS .tar filename with the following command or at the prompt. The **dir flash:** command will list the current IOS tar filename.

3750-S2# **copy flash:** [IOS filename] **tftp:**

Step 4: Verify the DRAM and Flash memory space available.

The **show version** command is used to verify the required DRAM memory is available for the IOS image file. The **dir flash:** command will verify there is enough Flash memory available for the IOS upgrade as well. Run both commands **on all** stacked switches to verify. The required DRAM/Flash memory for the IOS file was noted from the download page.

The network engineer has the options to add memory or delete files from Flash to provide enough space for the IOS image. Each hardware platform defines the maximum amount of supported DRAM and Flash memory. Where possible upgrade the memory required for either memory type. The network engineer can delete unused files from Flash as well where enough space isn't available. The following command will delete old Cisco IOS image file (.bin)

> 3750-S2# **delete flash:** [IOS filename]

The following command will delete a directory and all the files in the flash directory. This command is sometimes required where the previous command doesn't work.

> 3750-S2# **delete /force /recursive flash:** [dir_name]

Step 5: Copy the IOS image file to stack master switch

Log in to the **Master** switch through the switch console port or with a Telnet session and enter enable mode. There is an option as well to copy IOS image to USB stick. From there the IOS image file is copied from USB drive to switch Flash.

> 3750-S2# **copy tftp: flash:** [IOS filename]

Step 6: Extract the IOS image.tar file to all stack member switches

The following example retains the old IOS image on each switch member Verify connectivity to the TFTP server first with a ping first. Turn off desktop firewall temporarily if the ping isn't working. The following example extracts the IOS tar image to a switch stack with three member switches. The **archive download-sw** and **archive upload-sw** commands can only be used through the stack master switch.

3750-S2# **archive download-sw /destination-system 1 /destination-system 2 /destination-system 3 /reload tftp://**[ip address]/c3750-universalk9-mz.122-55.SE10.tar

switch# **archive download-sw** ?

/destination-system	specify destination system to receive software
/directory	specify a directory for images
/force-reload	unconditional reload after successful IOS upgrade
/force-ucode-reload	upgrade UCODE after successful IOS upgrade and before an unconditional reload
/imageonly	Load only the IOS image(s)
/leave-old-sw	Leave old sw installed after successful sw upgrade
/no-set-boot	Don't set BOOT -- leave existing boot config alone
/no-version-check	skip version check that prevents incompatible image install
/only-system-type	specify individual system type to be updated
/overwrite	OK to overwrite an existing image
/reload	Reload system (if no unsaved config changes) after successful upgrade
/safe	Always load before deleting old version
/upgrade-ucode	Upgrade UCODE after successful upgrade (no reload)
flash1:	Image file
flash2:	Image file
flash:	Image file
ftp:	Image file
http:	Image file
https:	Image file
rcp:	Image file
scp:	Image file
tftp:	Image file

Step 7: Verify the boot flash variable was updated

The boot variable from boot marker section is automatically updated for the startup configuration script. Issue the show boot command to verify the BOOT path-list will load the new image at the next switch reload.

> 3750-S2# **show boot**

BOOT path-list: flash:c3750-i5-mz.122-55.SE/c3750-i5-mz.122-55.SE.bin

Step 8: Save changes, reload and verify upgrade

The write mem command saves changes from running configuration script to the startup configuration. The reload will make the new IOS image active and show version command verifies the upgraded IOS version is running.

> 3750-S2# **write mem**
> 3750-S3# **reload**
> 3750-S2# **show version**

Manual IOS Upgrade (.tar)

The previous section of this document explained how to auto-upgrade an IOS tar file with the **archive download-sw** command. You can also upgrade the IOS manually switch-by-switch without disconnecting the stack cables. The following procedure details how to do a manual IOS upgrade with an IOS tar file image for 2960, 3560 and 3750 stack switches.

Summary Steps

Step 1: Select and download IOS image (.tar) file.
Step 2: Determine the stack master switch
Step 3: Backup the current IOS image to TFTP server
Step 4: Verify the DRAM and Flash memory space available.
Step 5: Copy the IOS tar image to stack master switch
Step 6: Extract the .tar file to stack switch members.
Step 7: Configure the boot flash variable at each switch
Step 8: Save changes, reload and verify upgrade

Step 1: Select and download the IOS image .tar file.

Go to www.cisco.com and select the IOS release version and feature set. Consider the guidelines from the "Selecting IOS Software " section for optimized selection. Download the corresponding .tar image file to the TFTP server. Note the DRAM and Flash memory required for the IOS image.

Step 2: Determine the stack master switch

The switch with the highest priority value is assigned master switch in a stack. Cisco recommends assigning priority value 15 to the switch preferred as stack master. The following **show switch** command example lists the priority settings for all switches as part of the stack. The designated master switch for the stack is switch 1:

3750-S1# **show switch**

Switch#	Role	Mac Address	Current Priority	State
*1	**Master**	0015.63f6.b700	15	Ready
2	Member	0015.c6c1.3000	10	Ready
3	Member	0015.c6c1.3000	9	Ready

Step 3: Backup the current IOS image to TFTP server

The best practice is to make a backup copy of the current IOS .tar image to TFTP server. That allows the network engineer to restore the current IOS image if there is a problem with the upgrade. The backup allows deletion of the current IOS file to increase Flash memory where required. Include the IOS .tar filename with the following command. The **dir flash:** command will list the current IOS tar filename.

3750-S1# **copy flash:** [IOS filename] **tftp:**

Step 4: Verify there is enough DRAM/Flash memory available

Verify there is enough DRAM and Flash memory available on the all stack switches. The DRAM memory available is verified with the **show version** command run at each switch. The available Flash memory is listed with the **dir flash**[x]**:** command. Add the switch number for each stack switch. For example **flash1:** for switch member 1. The master switch is **flash:** or the assigned stack number. The IOS image requires a minimum amount of DRAM system memory to load. In addition the switch requires enough Flash memory to store the IOS image file.

The network engineer has the option to upgrade DRAM and/or Flash memory required. Each hardware platform defines the maximum amount of upgradeable DRAM and Flash memory. The network engineer can delete any unused files from Flash as well where enough space isn't available. The master switch should have twice the amount of Flash memory of the .tar image file size. The Flash will store the .tar file and extracted files. For example, if the .tar image size is 5 MB, the minimum Flash space required is 10 MB. The following command deletes the current IOS file.

3750-S1# **delete flash:** [IOS filename.tar]

Note: The following optional command will delete the directory and files from Flash. That sometimes works where the previous command doesn't.

3750-S1# **delete /force /recursive flash:** [dir_name]

Step 5: Copy the .tar file to the master switch flash.

3750-S1# **copy tftp: flash:**

Address or name of remote host [] ? [TFTP Server IP Address]
Source filename [] ? c3750-universalk9-tar.122-55.SE10.tar
Destination filename [c3750- universalk9-tar.122-55.SE10.tar] ?

Step 6: Extract the .tar file to each stack switch member.

Extract the .tar images to the Flash memory of all switches. The command **archive tar /xtract** creates a directory to extract files under a new directory.

3750-S1# **archive tar /xtract** [tar file name] [extract directory]

1. Extract the .tar file to the Flash memory on switch 1 (master).

3750-S1# archive tar /xtract c3750-universalk9-tar.122-25.SEE1.tar flash1:

2. Extract the .tar file to the Flash memory of switch member 2.

3750-S2# archive tar /xtract c3750-universalk9-tar.122-25.SEE1.tar flash2:

3. Extract the .tar file to the Flash memory of switch member 3.

3750-S3# archive tar /xtract c3750-universalk9-tar.122-25.SEE1.tar flash3:

The **archive download-sw** command performs 3 steps during automatic IOS upgrade. The manual upgrade does each switch individually. For example, switch 1 is designated as the master switch while switch 2 and switch 3 are member switches.

Step 7: Configure the boot variable at each switch

After extracting the .tar files to the Flash of all stack switches, configure the boot variable at each switch to point to the new IOS image. Run the **dir** command to verify where the tar file was extracted. The directory name is specified with the **xtract** command. The default is to create a new directory with the same name as the tar image file. The **boot system switch all flash:** command is used to change the boot variable.

3750-S1# **dir**

c3750-universalk9-mz.122-25.SEE1.bin

3750-S1(config)# **boot system switch all flash:**/c3750-universalk9-mz.122-55.SE10.bin

Step 8: Save changes, reload switch and verify upgrade

Don't forget to save the changes to the startup configuration script with the **write mem** command. Reload the switch and verify the switch is running the new Cisco IOS software release.

3750-S1# **write mem**
3750-S1# **reload**

The **show version** command verifies the upgraded IOS version 12.2(25)S and feature set license (Universalk9) is now active. That includes the master switch (*1) and all stack members.

3750-S1# **show version**

Cisco IOS Software, C3750 Software (C3750-**UNIVERSALK9-M**), Version **12.2(55)SE10**, RELEASE SOFTWARE (fc1) Copyright (c) 1986-2006 by Cisco Systems, Inc. Compiled Mon 2-May-06 11:25
Image text-base: 0x00003000, data-base: 0x01255B58

Switch	Ports	Model	SW Version	SW Image
*1	28	WS-C3750X-24PS	12.2(55)SE10	C3750-Universalk9
2	52	WS-C3750X-48TS	12.2(55)SE10	C3750- Universalk9
3	26	WS-C3750X-24TS	12.2(55)SE10	C3750- Universalk9

3750-S1# **show switch**

Switch#	Role	Mac Address	Current Priority	State
*1	**Master**	0015.63f6.b700	15	Ready
2	Member	0015.c6c1.3000	10	Ready
3	Member	000f.f794.3d00	1	Ready

Manual IOS Upgrade (.bin)

The following describes the manual IOS upgrade of a 3750 switch stack with a .bin file. The auto-upgrade feature is only available with .tar images. The example has a switch stack with two switches and switch 2 assigned as the master switch.

Summary Steps

Step 1: Select and download the IOS image (.bin) file
Step 2: Determine the stack master switch
Step 3: Backup the current IOS image to TFTP server
Step 4: Verify the DRAM and Flash memory available
Step 5: Copy the IOS .bin image to all stack switches
Step 6: Configure the boot variable at each switch member
Step 7: Save changes, reload and verify upgrade

Step 1: Select and download new IOS .bin file with feature set license.

Go to www.cisco.com and select the IOS release version and feature set. Consider the guidelines from "Selecting IOS Software" section for optimized selection. Download the corresponding .bin image file to the TFTP server. Note the DRAM and Flash memory required for the IOS image.

Step 2: Determine the stack master switch

The switch with the highest priority value is assigned master switch in a stack. Cisco recommends assigning priority value 15 to the switch preferred as stack master. The **show switch** command lists the stack member priority settings and the designated master for the stack:

3750-S2# **show switch**

Switch#	Role	Mac Address	Current Priority	State
1	Member	0015.63f6.b700	5	Ready
*2	**Master**	0015.c6c1.3000	15	Ready

Step 3: Backup the current IOS image to TFTP server

The recommended best practice is to make a backup copy of the current IOS image to TFTP server. That allows the network engineer to restore the current IOS image if there is a problem with the upgrade. The backup allows deletion of the current IOS file to increase Flash memory where required as well. Include the IOS .bin filename with the following command or at the prompt. The **dir** command will list the current IOS bin filename on Flash.

> 3750-S2# **copy flash:** [IOS filename] **tftp:**

Step 4: Verify there is enough DRAM and Flash memory available

Verify there is enough DRAM and Flash memory available on the all switch stack members. The DRAM memory available is verified with the **show version** command run at each switch. The Flash memory available is listed with the **dir flash**[x]**:** command. Add the switch number for each stack member. For instance **flash1:** for switch member 1 and **flash2:** for the master switch.

> 3750-S1# **dir flash1:**
> 3750-S2# **dir flash2:**

The IOS image requires a minimum amount of DRAM system memory to load. In addition the switch requires enough Flash memory to store the IOS image file. The network engineer has the option to upgrade DRAM and/or Flash memory required. Each hardware platform defines the maximum amount of upgradeable DRAM and Flash memory. The network engineer can delete any unused files from Flash as well where enough space isn't available. The following command deletes the current IOS image file (.bin)

3750-S2# **delete flash:** [IOS filename.tar]

The following command will delete a directory and all the files in the flash directory. This command is sometimes required where the previous command doesn't work. The format flash: command will delete all files as well however not recommended.

3750-S2# **delete /force /recursive flash:** [dir]/[IOS filename]

Step 5: Copy IOS .bin file from TFTP server to each switch stack member

The following command will copy the .bin image from the TFTP server to the Flash memory of both stack switch members. The other options include RCP server or FTP server.

3750-S1# **copy tftp: flash1:**
3750-S2# **copy tftp: flash2:**

Step 6: Configure the boot variable at each stacked switch.

Configure the boot variable at each stacked switch with the following command to boot the new IOS image:

3750-S2(config)# **boot system switch all flash:/[IOS filename.bin]**
3750-S2(config)# **exit**
3750-S2# **write mem**
3750-S2# **show boot**

Master switch

BOOT path-list: flash:/c3750-universalk9-mz.122-55.SE10.bin

Switch 1
Member switch

BOOT path-list: flash:/c3750-universalk9-mz.122-55.SE10.bin

Step 7: Save changes, reload switch and verify upgrade

Save the changes to the startup configuration script with the **write mem** command. Reload the switch and verify the switch is running the new Cisco IOS software release. The **show version** command verifies the upgraded IOS version 12.2(55)SE10 and feature set license (Universalk9) is now active. That includes the master switch (*1) and all stack members.

> 3750-S2# **write mem**
>
> 3750-S2# **reload**
>
> 3750-S2# Proceed with reload? [confirm]

3750-S1# **show version**

Switch	Ports	Model	SW Version	SW Image
1	28	WS-C3750G-24PS	**12.2(55)SE10**	C3750-Universalk9
*2	52	WS-C3750G-48TS	**12.2(55)SE10**	C3750-Universalk9

3750-S1# **show switch**

Switch#	Role	Mac Address	Current Priority	State
1	Member	0015.63f6.b700	5	Ready
*2	**Master**	0015.c6c1.3000	10	Ready

Cisco ISR G2 Router IOS Upgrade

The Cisco ISR G2 router platforms run 15.x IOS code architecture. The Cisco newer 3560X and 3750X access switches however support both 12.x and 15.x IOS release versions. The following describes the procedure for upgrading IOS software on Cisco ISR G2 series routers. That includes the 1900, 2900 and 3900 series router models.

Summary Steps

Step 1: Backup the startup configuration file.

Step 2: Backup the current IOS image to TFTP server.

Step 3: Select and download the IOS image file.

Step 4: Verify the available DRAM and Flash memory.

Step 5: Copy the IOS system image to router flash memory.

Step 6: Configure the boot variable.

Step 7: Save changes, reload and verify upgrade.

Step 1: Backup the Startup Configuration File

The startup configuration contains the device configuration commands. It is loaded from NVRAM and becomes the running configuration script. Any changes saved with **write mem** or **copy run start** commands update the startup script. This is key so changes aren't lost when the device reboots.

It is a recommended to always backup the startup configuration file before making any change to a router. There are multiple options available to network engineers for file transfer. The supported destination include FTP server, TFTP server and RCP (Unix server). Refer to Cisco online documentation for server-side setup. The preferred method is to use SolarWinds or Cisco Prime Infrastructure for backup and restoring configuration scripts.

Backup Startup Configuration File (FTP and TFTP)

1. router > **enable**
2. router# **copy nvram:startup-config** [ftp: | tftp:]
3. router# **dir** [flash0: | flash1:]

Restore Startup Configuration File (FTP and TFTP)

1. router > **enable**
2. router# **copy** [ftp: | tftp:] **nvram:startup-config**
3. router# **dir** [flash0: | flash1:]

Backup Startup Configuration File from Router to RCP Server

```
router# conf t
router(config)# ip rcmd remote-username username
router(config)# end
router# copy nvram:startup-config rcp:
        [[[//[username@]location]/directory]/filename]
```

Restore Startup Configuration File from RCP Server to Router

```
router# conf t
router# ip rcmd remote-username  username
router# exit
router# copy rcp:
        [[[//[username@]location ]/directory ]/filename]
        system:startup-config
```

Step 2: Backup the IOS image file to TFTP server

The **copy flash: tftp:** command in Privileged EXEC mode will make a backup copy the current IOS system image to a TFTP server. This makes it easier to do a restore where necessary from the TFTP server. The IOS image can be copied to USB stick as well for backup purposes. The **show run** command will list the boot filename to backup. It is listed in the boot marker section on the running configuration script. In addition the **dir flash0:** command will list the current IOS image filename. That identifies the IOS boot file name when not specified in the running configuration. The Cisco ISR G2 supports two external Compact Flash (CF) slots for storing IOS images. The slot naming is flash: (or flash0:) and flash1: The following command copies the IOS image from flash0: however sometimes flash1: is used for storing IOS images.

```
router# dir flash0:
router# copy flash0: tftp:
Source filename ? [IOS filename]
Address or name of remote host [] ? 192.168.0.10
Destination filename [IOS filename] ? [IOS filename]
```

Step 3: Select and download the IOS image file

Go to www.cisco.com and select the IOS release version and feature set. Consider the guidelines from "Selecting IOS Software " section for optimized selection. Download the corresponding image file to the TFTP server. Note the required DRAM and Flash memory listed for the IOS image.

Step 4: Verify the DRAM and Flash memory available

The minimum requirements for the Cisco ISR G2 series router IOS images are 512 MB DRAM and 256 MB Flash memory. The **show version** command will list the available DRAM (processor memory). In addition the **dir flash:** command will list the available Flash space on the router.

The DRAM memory is used for running the IOS software while Flash memory stores the IOS image file. Compare what is available for each memory with the minimum requirement. Upgrade DRAM/Flash memory where required and/or delete files from Flash to proceed with the upgrade

> router# **show version**
> router# **dir flash0:**

This command displays all files and directories in Flash memory. Consider any files to delete including older IOS images not used. The network engineer could TFTP any files before deleting them as well. The files are erased with the **delete flash:** command specifying the directory and filename. Do not delete the current IOS image unless a backup is available.

> router# **dir /all flash0:**
> router# **delete flash0:**[directory/IOS filename]

Step 5: Copy the IOS image to Flash

The following describes how to TFTP the IOS image to the router compact flash memory. There is an option to use RCP as well with copy rcp: flash0:

> router# **copy tftp: flash0:**

Step 6: Configure the boot variable

The network engineer must edit the boot system command for the new IOS filename. The startup configuration will point to the IOS image specified with the boot system command. The router would load the first IOS image listed in Flash when there is no boot system specified. The alternate option is to delete any older IOS image files from Flash after the IOS upgrade is verified with a router restart. The new IOS image would then load as a result.

> router# **conf t**
> router (config)# **boot system flash0:** [IOS filename]

Step 7: Save changes, reload and verify upgrade

The configuration changes are saved to the startup configuration file with write mem command and reloaded. The **show version** command verifies router was upgraded to the new IOS release version and feature set license.

> router# **write mem**
> router# **reload**
> router# **show version**

Cisco 3650/3850 IOS-XE Upgrade

The newer Cisco IOS-XE builds on the traditional IOS software to provide platform independent code. The IOS-XE image is comprised of IOS release 15.0 with XE code for platform abstraction. The Catalyst 3650, Catalyst 3850 and ASR routers run on IOS-XE software. The migration to IOS-XE architecture is the next generation IOS software code platform for Cisco equipment. The traditional IOS runs as a separate process with the new architecture enabling the following

Features

- Hardware driver platform abstraction (independent)
- Control Plane and Data Plane Separation
- Multi-core CPU load balancing
- Easier new application integration
- Upgrading Cisco IOS XE Software

The procedure for upgrading the Catalyst 3650 and 3850 series switches are determined by the switch boot mode. The initial setup and configuration of the switches allows for selecting an IOS boot mode. The Catalyst 3650 and 3850 switches run IOS XE software that supports install and bundle boot modes.

Switch Boot Modes

The Cisco recommendation is to use the default Install mode for optimized boot features and less memory required. The install IOS image is comprised of a package-provisioning file (packages.conf) and multiple package files (.pkg) stored on the flash memory. The purpose of the packages.conf file is to govern the switch boot. The packages.conf file is created automatically during the install process.

The bundle mode option is similar to the traditonal IOS boot process with a single IOS file. The bundle mode option extracts the packages from the Bundle and copies them to switch memory (DRAM). That will increase the amount of memory required for upgrade and time required to boot. The procedures for the following configurations are described.

- Upgrading Cisco IOS XE Software: Install Mode
- Upgrading Cisco IOS XE Software: Bundle Mode
- Upgrading Cisco IOS XE Software: Stack

IOS-XE Install Mode Upgrade

The IOS-XE software install privileged EXEC command install the packages from a new IOS software bundle file. The software bundle can be installed from the flash, USB stick or installed over the network using TFTP or FTP. The software install command expands the package files from the bundle file and copies them to the switch flash memory. The network method downloads the bundle file directly to switch DRAM. The package files are expanded and copied to switch flash and the running provisioning file (packages.conf) is updated to reference the new IOS packages. Booting the switch from USB (usbflash0:) or TFTP server is not supported with install mode configured. The following is the install mode upgrade procedure.

Step 1: Verify the switch boot mode is install.
Step 2: Select and download the IOS-XE image file.
Step 3: Verify the DRAM and Flash memory available.
Step 4: Copy the IOS-XE image file to flash memory.
Step 5: Run the software install command.
Step 6: Reload the switch.

Step 1: Verify the switch boot mode is install

As mentioned there are two separate upgrade procedures that are selected based on the switch boot mode configured. The network engineer must verify the switch is running Install mode before proceeding with the install oriented upgrade. That is accomplished with the **show version** command.

C3850-S1# **show version**

Switch	Ports	Model	SW Version	SW Image	Mode
*1	32	WS-C3850-24T	03.03.03SE	cat3k_caa-universalk9	INSTALL

Verify Cisco IOS XE provisioning file (packages.conf) and location on switch flash with the following command. Specifies information on the Cisco IOS XE package files currently running. This is typically the set of packages listed in the booted provisioning file.

Step 2: Select and download the IOS-XE image file

Go to www.cisco.com and select the IOS release version and feature set. Consider the guidelines from "Selecting IOS Software " section for optimized selection. Download the corresponding .bin image file to the TFTP server. The 3650 and 3850 series switches do not support tar files. Note the required DRAM and Flash memory listed for the IOS image.

Step 3: Verify the DRAM and Flash memory available

The **show version** command will list the available DRAM memory for the switch. In addition the **dir flash:** command will verify the available Flash memory. The switch must have a greater amount of memory available than IOS image size.

> 3850-S1# **dir flash:**
> 3850-S1# **show version**

Step 4: Copy the IOS-XE image file to switch Flash memory.

The install mode requires the IOS package files to be copied to the switch Flash. The IOS image file is copied from TFTP server to the switch Flash memory. In addition there is support for copying the IOS file from a USB stick (usbflash0:) to flash. It is easier and faster where possible to copy from USB to flash with copy **usbflash0: flash:** command.

> 3850-S1# **copy tftp: flash:**

For usbflash0: the default format is FAT16, while FAT32 format is also supported with IOS release 15.1 for some hardware platforms.

> 3850-S1# **format usbflash0:**

> FAT16 filesystem type = 1 GB USB, 2 GB USB
> FAT32 filesystem type = 4 GB USB (IOS 15.1)

Step 5: Run the software install command

The NEW keyword renames the old package file set for rollback purpose. Without this, the post-install package set merges the current package and the new package set. The supported IOS file source includes flash memory, usbflash0: or network tftp, ftp or http.

Obtain the IOS filename from flash with **dir flash:** command (privileged EXEC mode). The boot variable is changed to point to the "packages.conf" file for the switch.

3850-S1# **dir flash:**

Directory of flash:/

24531 -rwx 220716072 Oct 10 2014 12:55:59 +00:00 cat3k_caa-universalk9.SSA.03.08.88.EMP.150-8.88.EMP.bin

3850-S1# **software install file** [source] [filename.bin] **new**

3850-S1# **software install file flash**:cat3k_caa-universalk9.SSA.03.08.88.EMP.150-8.88.EMP.bin

[1]: Creating pending provisioning file
[1]: Finished installing software. New software will load on reboot.
[1]: Committing provisioning file
[1]: Do you want to proceed with reload? [yes/no]:

This example shows the software install file command being used to expand and copy the packages from a Cisco IOS XE bundle located on a TFTP server in order to upgrade to a new image:

3850-S1# **software install file tftp:**//172.16.21.25/cat3k_caa-universalk9.SSA.03.12.02.EZP.150-12.02.EZP.150-12.02.EZP.bin

Preparing install operation

[1]: Downloading file tftp://172.16.21.25/cat3k_caa-universalk9.SSA.03.12.02.EZP.150-12.02.EZP.150-12.02.EZP.bin to active switch 1
[1]: Finished downloading file tftp://172.16.21.25/cat3k_caa-universalk9.SSA.03.12.02.EZP.150-12.02.EZP.150-12.02.EZP.bin to active switch 1
[1]: Starting install operation
[1]: Expanding bundle cat3k_caa-universalk9.SSA.03.12.02.EZP.150-12.02.EZP.150-12.02.EZP.bin
[1]: Copying package files
[1]: Package files copied
[1]: Finished expanding bundle cat3k_caa-universalk9.SSA.03.12.02.EZP.150-12.02.EZP.150-12.02.EZP.bin
[1]: Verifying and copying expanded package files to flash:
[1]: Verified and copied expanded package files to flash:
[1]: Starting compatibility checks

[1]: Finished compatibility checks
[1]: Starting application pre-installation processing
[1]: Finished application pre-installation processing
[1]: Old files list:
Removed cat3k_caa-base.SSA.03.09.17.EMP.pkg
Removed cat3k_caa-drivers.SSA.03.09.17.EMP.pkg
Removed cat3k_caa-infra.SSA.03.09.17.EMP.pkg
Removed cat3k_caa-iosd-universalk9.SSA.150-9.17.EMP.pkg
Removed cat3k_caa-platform.SSA.03.09.17.EMP.pkg
Removed cat3k_caa-wcm.SSA.03.09.17.EMP.pkg
[1]: New files list:
Added cat3k_caa-base.SPA.03.02.00.SE.pkg
Added cat3k_caa-drivers.SPA.03.02.00.SE.pkg
Added cat3k_caa-infra.SPA.03.02.00SE.pkg
Added cat3k_caa-iosd-universalk9.SPA.150-1.EX.pkg
Added cat3k_caa-platform.SPA.03.02.00.SE.pkg
Added cat3k_caa-wcm.SPA.03.02.00.SE.pkg
[1]: Creating pending provisioning file
[1]: Finished installing software. New software will load on reboot.
[1]: Setting rollback timer to 45 minutes
[1]: Do you want to proceed with reload? [yes/no]:

Step 6: Reload the switch

     3850-S1# **reload**

Cisco IOS XE Bundle Mode Upgrade

The bundle mode upgrade requires copying the IOS XE bundle (.bin file) to the switch flash or USB (usbflash0:). To list the Cisco IOS XE bundle (.bin file) or each IOS XE package (.pkg) file use the show software package command. The following describes the procedure for upgrading Cisco IOS XE software when the switch is in bundle mode.

    Step 1: Verify the switch boot mode is bundle
    Step 2: Select IOS-XE bundle file and download to TFTP server.
    Step 3: Verify the DRAM and Flash memory available.
    Step 4: Copy bundle file (.bin) to switch flash
    Step 5: Configure boot system command.
    Step 6: Save changes, reload and verify upgrade

Step 1: Verify the switch boot mode is bundle.

> 3650-S1# **show version**

Step 2: Select and download IOS-XE file to TFTP server or USB stick.

Step 3: Verify the DRAM and Flash memory available.

> 3650-S1# **dir flash:**
> 3650-S1# **show version**

Step 4: Copy the bundle file (.bin) to flash memory.

3650-S1# **copy tftp:**//172.16.21.25/cat3k_caa-universalk9.SSA.03.12.02.EZP.150-12.02.EZP.150-12.02.EZP.bin **flash:**

Destination filename [cat3k_caa-universalk9.SSA.03.12.02.EZP.150-12.02.EZP.150-12.02.EZP.bin]?

Step 5: Configure the boot variable

The IOS-XE bundle mode requires configuration of the boot variable. The boot variable for the switch should point to the upgraded IOS image file.

> 3650-S1# **conf t**
> 3650-S1 (config)# **boot system switch all flash:**cat3k_caa-universalk9.SSA.03.12.02.EZP.150-12.02.EZP.150-12.02.EZP.bin

Step 6: Save changes, reload and verify upgrade

The configuration changes are saved to the startup configuration file with write mem command and restarted with the reload command. The **show version** command verifies the switch was upgraded to the new IOS release version and feature set license.

> 3850-S1(config)# **exit**
> 3850-S1# **write mem**
> 3850-S1# **reload**
> 3850-S1# **show version**

Catalyst 3650/3850 Switch Stack Upgrade

The following describe the IOS upgrade options for the Catalyst 3650 and 3850 series stacked switches.

Auto Upgrade (IOS-XE 3.6+)

The Auto-Upgrade feature is available with any switch stack running install boot mode and IOS-XE version 3.6 or later.

Step 1: Configure the **software auto-upgrade enable** global command on the master switch. Run the **write mem** command to save changes.

Step 2: Connect the new switch to the stack and power it on.

Step 3: The switch is automatically upgraded with IOS-XE version 3.6 or later and reloads.

Step 4: Verify the new switch is now running the upgraded IOS-XE code using the **show version** command.

Step 5: (Optional Method) Run **show switch** command to determine the switch with the older IOS-XE version and do the following.

> 3850-S1# **software auto-upgrade**
> 3850-S1# **reload slot** [switch member number]

3850 Stack Manual Upgrade

The manual upgrade is available with any IOS-XE version release. The following describes the procedure for doing an IOS manual upgrade.

Step 1: Copy the IOS-XE image file to Flash with TFTP, USB or Telnet

> 3850-S1# **copy tftp: flash:**

Step 2: The **software install file flash** command copies the IOS image from the current switch to all stack members. The **switch 1-2** command unpacks bin file to each switch and installs the software.

> 3850-S1# **software install file flash:** [filename] [switch 1-2]

Step 3: Reload the switch and verify upgrade

> 3850-S1# **reload**
> 3850-S1# **show version**

Installing Feature Licenses

The Universal IOS file image is a key aspect of the new software licensing architecture now available. The Universal IOS image contains all Cisco IOS feature set packages. The previous delivery model was based on separate IOS files for every feature package available. The features are enabled with software licenses downloaded online from Cisco. The Universal image is supported with 1900, 2900 and 3900 series ISR G2 routers and most Catalyst switches. The Catalyst 6500 and Catalyst 4900 series switches do not support Universal images. The two versions of Universal images include IOS image file with payload encryption and no payload encryption.

Payload Encryption (K9)

Universal images with the "universalk9" designation in the image name provide strong crypto features such as VPN payload, SSL and Secure UC. The universal image offers all the Cisco IOS feature set packages as well.

No Payload Encryption (NPE)

Universal images with the universalk9_npe" designation in the image name do not provide encryption features. Some countries do not permit any strong crypto features in any form. The universal image with NPE designator is selected to allow for the export of IOS software.

Feature License Models

Cisco currently supports two feature set licensing models for the supported Catalyst switches and routers. They are software activation and right-to-use license models.

Software Activation Feature License

These are standard upgrades to technology feature package licenses included on new router shipments or upgrade through Cisco Software Activation. The licenses are enforced as well with Cisco Software Licensing model. The customer can enable some individual features as well. These features verify the permanent feature set package license is present before enabling. For example CME-SRST is an individual feature license that requires the UC technology package with encryption (UCK9).

Right to Use Feature License (RTU)

The RTU licenses is based on the traditional licensing model where there is no software activation available. The feature set licenses are ordered when the router is shipped or at a later date. The Catalyst 3850 series switches use Right-to-Use licensing.

Cisco License Types

Permanent

The Permanent License never expires and once installed is enabled across all IOS versions and upgrades. The permanent license is the standard license type for IOS Technology Packages (IP Base, UC, SEC, DATA) and individual Feature Licenses such as SSL VPN, AppX etc.

Temporary

The Temporary License is enabled for a limited trial period. The ISR G2 router includes 60 day Temporary Licenses for the Data, UC and Security feature set packages. The Temporary License is often used for customer consideration before upgrading to a Permanent License. There is no extension allowed after expiry date. Cisco Technical Assistance Center (TAC) will activate a new temporary license for troubleshooting purposes.

Counted License

Counted licenses is based on a permitted number of user connections. Some examples include CME User Licenses or number of SSL VPN connections per router. The Software Activation Licensing enabled easier management of user count licenses.

Subscription License

The Subscription License provides access to services or features for a specified period of time. The License can be extended with a renewal for a new fixed time period. The URL Filtering and Web Application Firewall (WAF) are examples of a Subscription License. There are regular updates often from a cloud service.

Feature Set Packages

The Universal image is comprised of all available feature set packages. The ISR G2 router platform has been consolidated to four primary packages that include IP Base, DATA, UC (Unified Communications) and SEC (Security). The Universal image as a result enables Software Activation Licensing. Each license key is assigned to a particular device. It is obtained from Cisco by providing the product ID and serial number of the router and a Product Activation Key (PAK) after purchase. In addition Cisco would install license keys for paid software before shipping. The feature license packages from Table 2-1 compare legacy and equivalent current packages. The Universal feature set includes all individual packages for encryption (k9) and npe.

Table 2-1 Comparison of Legacy and ISR Next Generation Feature Set

ISR Legacy Feature Set	ISR G2 Feature Set
IP Base	IP Base
IP Voice	UC
Enterprise Base	DATA
Enterprise Services	DATA + UC
SP Services	DATA + UC
Advanced Security	SEC
Advanced IP Services	SEC + UC + DATA
Advanced Enterprise Services	SEC + UC + DATA

Software Activation License (SAL)

The Software Activation License provided by Cisco for the device includes Device Product ID, Device Serial Number and Product Activation Key (PAK).

Product ID + Serial Number + PAK = Software Activation License (SAL)

The new feature package is enabled with a Software Activation License for the IOS Universal image. The SAL is a unique to the switch or router and not transferable. The technology package or individual feature license set is purchased with a Product Activation Key (PAK). The Software Activation License is an XML text file with a .lic extension.

Software Activation licenses other than IP Base feature set, must be transferred from the failed device to a replacement device (RMA) for all license features enabled the replacement router. The Product ID and Serial Number of failed device is used to transfer licenses to replacement device through the Cisco licensing portal.

Step-by-Step Procedure

The following steps outline how to install Software Activation licenses for feature upgrades. The technology packages (i.e Data, UC, SEC) and ordering SKU vary among hardware platforms. The following example is based on the Cisco ISR G2 routers.

Step 1: Select and Order Cisco Technology Package

The Product ID (PID) and Serial Number (SN) for a device creates a Unique Device Identifier (UDI) assigned to a Cisco device. The Serial Number is an 11 digit number while the Product ID identifies the device type. The UDI is listed with "show license UDI" command from CLI. The device pull-out label tray lists the UDI as well. Drop the "V01" designator with the Product ID (i.e "CISCO3945/K9" instead of "CISCO3945/K9 V01).

Step 2: Order Product Authorization Key (PAK)

The Product Authorization Key (PAK) is an 11 digit alphanumeric key sent to the customer after purchasing the license. The PAK is used for generating software licenses on supported switches and routers. The new license is required to add any new feature set package or individual feature licenses. The PAK is assigned to a specific device when used to create a software activation license (SAL).

The PAK is sent to customers as paper-based or electronic delivery. The ordering SKU for the ISR paper PAK start with SL for technology package licenses and FL for specific feature licenses (Appx). In addition the paper PAK includes a software claim certificate identifying the PAK string.

The electronic PAK (E-PAK) is emailed to the customer online. The SKU for ISR E-PAK technology package licenses start with L-SL and L-FL for feature licenses. Customers selecting an electronic PAK receive an email that point to a secure portal where a PDF is downloaded with the PAK information. For example, customers upgrading from the IP Base to DATA technology package feature set require a new Software Activation License. Upgrading IOS software images from one release to another does not require a new license. The following E-PAK example is for the 3900 ISR G2 router DATA feature set package.

> SKU: L-SL-39-DATA-K9
> Product Qty: 1
> Product Authorization Key: [xxxxxxxxxxx]

Step 3: Generate License File Online

Access the Cisco licensing portal at www.cisco.com/go/license and provide the PAK, Serial Number and Product ID of the device. That generates a unique license file for the device that can be downloaded or emailed to you. There are three primary methods for generating and managing the software activation licenses. They include Cisco Product Licensing Registration Portal, IOS Call Home and Cisco License Manager (CLM)

Figure 2-7 Cisco License File

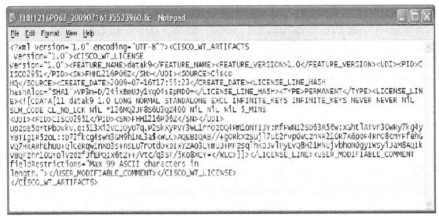

Method 1: Cisco Product Licensing Registration Portal

The Cisco Licensing Portal is available online for all license management activities. That includes ordering, converting, installing and transferring feature licenses. In addition temporary license requests are made available as well. The Software Activation License is examined by Cisco IOS Software after the install, to activate the appropriate feature sets.

Step 1: Sign on with Cisco username and password at:

www.cisco.com/en/us/partner/ordering/index.shtml

Step 2: Order the 11 digit ID PAK for feature set license upgrade online and delivered by mail or e-delivery.

Step 3: Obtain device serial number and PID with the following command or obtain from the router label tray.

router# **show license udi**

Step 4: Generate license file (.lic) from Cisco Licensing Portal at www.cisco.com/go/license.

- Enter all PAKs and click submit
- Enter the product ID and serial number of device.
- Add registration and end user information then submit.
- Download the license file online from Cisco.com by clicking "Download License" or email attachment sent from Cisco.

Step 5: Copy License File (.lic) to the device with the following command.

router# **copy tftp: flash0:**

Step 6: Install the new license file to the device with the following command.

router# **license install flash0:** [license_filename.lic]

Method 2: Cisco IOS Call Home

The Call Home option allows customers to access the Cisco Product License Registration portal directly from the CLI. The same features are available to generate, convert, install and manage feature licenses. Each transaction requires a new connection to the Cisco licensing portal.

Step 1: Order the suitable PAK from Cisco.
Step 2: Download and install the license

The license is installed with the **license call-home install pak** command. Select SKU(s), add user details to download / install license automatically.

device# **license call-home install pak** [number]

Pak Number : [xxxxxxxxxxx]
Pak Fulfillment type: PARTIAL
SKU Name : L-2900-LIC
SKU Type : NOMAPPING
Description : L-2900-LIC :
Ordered Qty : 1
Platform Supported : N/A

SKU Name : L-29-DATA-K9
SKU Type : Feature
Description : L-29-DATA-K9 :
Ordered Qty : 1
Available Qty : 1
Feature List :
Feature name: datak9 Count: Uncounted
Platform Supported : N/A
Select SKU to install [1-1] or Quit: 1
Selected SKU is : L-29-DATA-K9
Enter the user's detail:

1/1 licenses were successfully installed
0/1 licenses were existing licenses
0/1 licenses were failed to install

Method 3: Cisco License Manager (CLM)

The Cisco License Manager (CLM) is a client/server application for managing enterprise network licensing. The CLM is based on a license agent embedded in the Cisco IOS image at each device. That provides an automated discovery of feature licenses across the network. The results are saved to the Cisco managed licensing server. The communication between customer device agents and Cisco servers is with a secure encrypted connection across the internet.

Step 1: Apply for Cisco account privilege to launch CLM.

Step 2: Launch License Assistant wizard.

Step 3: Select PAKs (SKU) and the targeted devices.

Step 4: CLM downloads the license and install it automatically.

Step 5: Run CLM auto-discover for the customer.

Step 6: Install the license on the device and reboot to upgrade features.

Figure 2-8 Cisco License Manager (CLM)

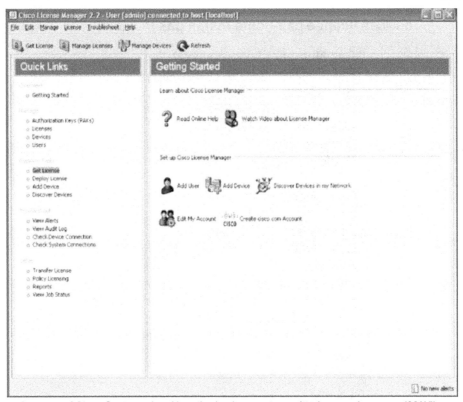

Courtesy of Cisco Systems, Inc. Unauthorized use not permitted, www.cisco.com (09/15)

Cisco Catalyst 3850 RTU Licensing

The Cisco Catalyst 3850 series switches use a trust-based licensing model. The upgrade of a feature set license is done from the switch CLI instead of a PAK. The IOS license commands are entered and accepts the EULA to activate the license instead of a product activation key (PAK). The customer would order the license from Cisco or a third party provider. The license is sent as E-delivery or mailed to them as proof of purchase. The upgrade options include IP Base and IP services. The default is LAN Base unless the customer orders an upgrade to ship with the switch. All feature set packages are shipped with the switch for activation. In addition all stacked switches must run same license level. The following commands are entered at the switch CLI for activating permanent and evaluation license types.

Permanent License:

3850# **license right-to-use activate** lanbase | ipbase | ipservices [slot #] **acceptEULA**

Evaluation License:

3850# **license right-to-use activate** ipbase | ipservices **evaluation** [slot #] **acceptEULA**

3850# **reload**

or 3850# **reload** [slot number] (stack member number)

Chapter 3

Configuration Fundamentals

Overview

The purpose of IOS software is to allow for configuration and management of network devices. The startup configuration script is comprised of multiple lines of command syntax. The configuration script is loaded from NVRAM to system memory (DRAM) to activate any enabled features and interfaces. The configuration of the network device is based on design requirements with command syntax that varies between software platforms.

The features and command syntax is based on the IOS release version. In addition upgrading IOS software is done to enable new features, support new hardware or fix bugs. This chapter discusses the configuration fundamentals starting with device connectivity. The configuration modes are explained and initial setup commands. There are additional sections for configuring interfaces, switching, routing, device management and security. Typical IOS troubleshooting techniques are included as well.

Connectivity Options

Terminal Emulation Software

The network devices are managed with terminal emulation software. There are various terminal emulation clients available for accessing Cisco switches, routers, firewalls and wireless devices. The most popular clients include PuTTY and Secure CRT. PuTTY is freeware while Secure CRT is available with additional features as shareware (paid). Both terminal clients support Telnet and SSH connectivity for remote connectivity to network devices. In addition there is console access for local connection. The console is typically used when doing the initial device configuration.

Figure 3-1 PuTTY Terminal Emulation Software

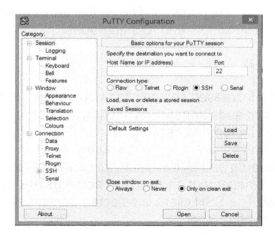

Console Port

The Cisco console port is available for connecting the network engineer laptop to the network device. It is a serial interface with an RJ45 style connector and used typically for initial device configuration or IOS upgrade. The default settings for the console port include 9600 bps, no parity, 8 data bits, 1 stop bit and no flow control. Configure the laptop side serial interface to match the same settings. The newer laptops do not provide traditional serial interfaces anymore. Instead the USB port is available with a USB to serial style cable. The serial end of that cable plugs into the cisco standard console cable with the RJ45 connector. The default terminal emulation settings often work with cisco devices however the network engineer can select something else. The network engineer would select serial client type when setting up the profile.

Figure 3-2 Connectivity to Cisco ISR Router Console Port

ISR G2 Router

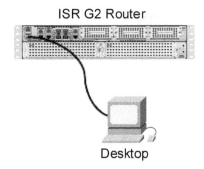

Desktop

Remote Telnet

The purpose of Telnet is to provide remote connectivity to a network device. The network device is assigned an IP management address with Telnet access enabled. The network engineer would select the telnet client option during the profile setup. The IP address or hostname is provided and any additional terminal features required. The typical telnet activities include troubleshooting, editing scripts and IOS upgrades.

Secure Shell (SSH)

The requirement for increased security has popularized SSH as a remote client. The SSH client adds transaction security with session encryption for all packets between laptop and network device. The management of network devices involve traversing the company WAN and sometimes public internet. The passwords and all device script configuration is encrypted as a result. The same management and support activities are performed with SSH as with Telnet. The SSH client is selected during setup of the connect profile with the encryption level.

Configuration Modes

The device configuration starts with getting to a CLI command prompt to enter commands. The CLI is an acronym for command line interface contrasted with the web GUI interface that is available as well. The network device whether it is a switch, router, firewall or wireless access point will step through a boot process when started. The following describe the configuration modes available and how to move between them.

User EXEC

The initial access is called User Exec and known with the router > style prompt. This access mode allows connectivity, changing terminal settings and some basic show commands for troubleshooting.

    switch >

Privileged EXEC

The Privileged Exec mode is password protected and permits access to all commands for editing device scripts. In addition all show commands are available from this mode as well. The network engineer would enter the **enable** command from User Exec mode and configured enable password.

    router > **enable**
    router#

Global Configuration Mode

There is a hierarchy to cisco IOS commands that include sub-commands as well. That applies to configuration commands or show commands. The show commands provide information on device system status, connectivity and script details. The network engineer would enter config t command at the Privileged Exec prompt to enter global configuration mode where config is denoted. From there the network engineer can enter global commands or proceed to subcommand modes for interface commands. The hostname command is a common global command for assigning a device name. To go up to the previous level type exit at any point. Multiple exit command are required when working from the sub-command level.

    router# **conf t**
    router(config)# **hostname** [hostname]

ROMmon Mode

During the boot process, any network device will attempt to load the IOS system image. The router will enter ROM monitor (ROMmon) mode if no system image is available or corrupt. The ROMmon mode is available as well by interrupting the boot sequence during startup with Ctrl-C sequence. The Break method does vary between device platforms and must occur during the first 60 seconds. The router will arrive at the rommon1> prompt where diagnostic tests and configuration changes can be performed. The ROMmon mode (or **switch:** prompt for switches) is most often used for troubleshooting purposes and password recovery.

    rommon1>

Setup Mode

Setup mode is commonly used as a facility for initial device configuration. The Cisco network device with no configuration starts and prompts the network engineer to enter basic information for router connectivity. The System Configuration Dialog provides multiple questions during the configuration process. That would start with some global commands and onto interface setup. The setup mode is available using the Setup command from Privileged EXEC mode as well after the device has been configured. The reset of the Cisco device to default settings will prompt the setup mode.

    router> **enable**
    Password: [password]
    router# **setup**

    --- System Configuration Dialog ---

    At any point you may enter a question mark '?' for help.
    Use ctrl-c to abort configuration dialog at any prompt.
    Default settings are in square brackets '[]'.

    Would you like to enter the initial configuration dialog? [yes/no]:

Configuration Submodes

The configuration submode is any configuration mode that is below global configuration mode. That would include multiple submodes such as interface configuration mode and subinterface configuration mode.

    router(config-if)# interface commands
    router(config-subif)# subinterface commands
    router(config-crypto-map)# crypto map commands
    router(config-ext-nacl)# extended ACL commands

Router and Switch Commands

The device configuration starts with global configuration commands. The device script is created based on design requirements. The changes are saved to the startup configuration script with **write mem** command from the enable prompt. That is shown with the hostname command. The bolded items are Cisco IOS commands with bracketed text for variable options. The standard configuration commands are all available with IOS 12.0 and 15.0 release versions for supported Catalyst switches and routers.

Software Platform: *Standard IOS*

Hardware Platforms:

- *Cisco Catalyst 2960, 3500 and 3750 Series Switches*
- *Cisco 1900, 2900 and 3900 ISR G2 Series Routers*

Global Configuration Mode

The following commands describe how to enter enable mode and global configuration mode. The enable password (if set) is required to enter global configuration mode.

```
device> enable
device# show ?
device# conf t
device(config)# global commands
device(config)# exit
device# write mem
```

Initial Setup Commands

The following are standard IOS commands used with the initial switch and router configuration. The global commands are standard with deployment of most network switches and routers for enterprise connectivity.

Hostname

The hostname command assigns a device name to the switch or router. The enable prompt will change to the assigned name at that point. The naming conventions are used for management and troubleshooting purposes.

```
router > enable
router# conf t
router(config)# hostname [R1]
R1(config)# exit
```

Service Timestamps

The service timestamps command enable all timestamp options for debugging and logging activities. The timestamps are added to the log files for troubleshooting purposes.

R1(config)# **service timestamps debug datetime localtime show-timezone**
R1(config)# **service timestamps log datetime localtime show-timezone**

IOS Boot System File

This command assigns the default IOS image filename (.bin or .tar) for boot purposes. This would point to the upgraded IOS image file on the device flash. There is a boot marker section as part of the startup configuration file where the command is added. Some automatic IOS upgrades will update the boot variable automatically. The examples include the IOS syntax for both routers and Catalyst switches.

R1(config)# **boot system flash flash0:** [IOS filename]
SW1(config)# **boot flash:**[/IOS filename]

Clock Timezone

Set the time zone for display, with the clock timezone command. To set the time to Coordinated Universal Time (UTC) use the no form of the command. The timezone works with the NTP server to provide accurate timestamps.

R1(config)# **clock timezone** [zone] [hours-offset] [minutes-offset]

Banner

This command will configure a banner notice for the company when a user logs on to the device. The typical purpose is to notify all users they should sign-off if they are not an authorized user.

R1(config)# **banner motd #** [type banner text]

DNS Domain Name

The default DNS domain name is configured for the switch or router with the following command. The company would define the domain name with the DNS architecture.

R1(config)# **ip domain-name** [company.domain.com]

IP Name Server

This global command is used to configure a DNS name server. The purpose of the DNS server is host name to IP address resolution.

    switch(config)# **ip name-server** [ip address]

DHCP Server

The following commands will configure a DHCP pool on a router. The router is assigned as a DHCP server to distribute IP addresses to network clients. The end user is assigned an IP address when connecting to the network. The DHCP pool is configured to allow IP addresses from a permitted range.

    router(config)# **service dhcp**
    router(config)# **ip dhcp pool** [name]
    router(dhcp-config)# **network** [ip address] [subnet mask]
    router(dhcp-config)# **dns-server** [ip address]
    router(dhcp-config)# **domain-name** [domain name]
    router(dhcp-config)# **default-router** [ip address]

IP Classless

The ip classless command enables selection of the most specific route from the routing table to any destination. The CIDR variable subnet prefixes are supported to allow optimized route selection.

    router(config)# **ip classless**

System Management

The following commands will setup standard system management for access to network devices, SNMP and event logging. In addition there is NTP for clock synchronization.

VTY Lines

The VTY lines enable remote Telnet access to switches and routers. That allows network engineer to configure the devices across the network. The commands enable login to VTY lines with a password for security purposes

    router(config)# **line vty** [0 4]
    router(config-line)# **password** [password]
    router(config-line)# **login**

Secure Shell (SSH)

The Secure Shell (SSH) provides a secure encrypted connection to the network device not available with Telnet. It is becoming mandatory for security compliance requirements to encrypt the connection to network devices. The key size is variable for additional encryption of packets.

> router(config)# **crypto key generate rsa general-keys modulus** [key size]
> router(config)# **ip ssh time-out** [60]
> router(config)# **ip ssh version 2**
> router(config)# **line vty** [0 4]
> router(config-line)# **transport input ssh telnet**

SNMP Community Strings

The SNMP protocol sends device status data (traps) to a network management station (NMS). The following commands enable SNMP for switches and routers. In addition the community string is a password that permits RO (read only) and RW (read write) access for the NMS to MIB (data). Enabling SNMP with community strings permits the management software package (NMS) to monitor and run performance reports.

> router(config)# **snmp-server community** [string] **RO**
> router(config)# **snmp-server community** [string] **RW**

System Logging

The logging command enables sending messages to a syslog server. The host-name is name or IP address of host assigned as a syslog server. The logging of system messages is a foundational part of the company network management strategy.

> router(config)# **logging** [host-name]

NTP Server

This command allows the device software clock to be synchronized by a Network Time Protocol (NTP) time server. The IP address or hostname of the time server provides clock synchronization. The clock source and synchronization is required for a variety of networking features.

> router(config)# **ntp server** [ip-address] [hostname]

Network Interfaces

The configuration of standard network interfaces is shared for Catalyst switches and routers. The switches are most often Ethernet interfaces while routers include both Ethernet and WAN interfaces.

Layer 3 Routed Interface

The following series of commands will configure a Layer 3 (routed) interface on an Ethernet switch port. The interface command starts the interface subcommand mode. For instance the network engineer could configure gigabitethernet0/1 as a routed interface. The slot designator is "0" and "1" is the port number. The newer 10 GE interfaces use tengigabitethernet0/1 syntax. The IP address and subnet mask is then assigned to the interface.

        switch(config)# **interface** [slot/port]
        switch(config-if)# **description** [text string]
        switch(config-if)# **ip address** [ip address] [subnet mask]

Switched Virtual Interface (SVI)

The SVI is a layer 3 interface configured on a Catalyst switch port for VLAN routing. The SVI enables Inter-VLAN routing with an entry to the routing table. The interfaces for users and devices assigned to the VLAN use the SVI as a routing gateway. The following command enables routing on the switch and assigns an IP address to the created VLAN.

        switch(config)# **ip routing**
        switch(config)# **vlan** [vlan number]
        switch(config)# **interface vlan** [vlan number]
        switch(config-if)# **ip address** [ip address] [subnet mask]

Switch Management Interface

The management subnet separates management and data traffic.
The standard for Catalyst switches is to create a management interface with an IP address assigned to any unused VLAN instead of the default VLAN 1. The purpose of VLAN 1 is to forward untagged control traffic between switches. The security best practice is to assign the management VLAN from the default VLAN 1 to any unused VLAN.

        switch(config)# **interface vlan** [255]
        switch (config-if)# **ip address** [ip address] [subnet mask]

Loopback Interface

The loopback is a virtual Layer 3 interface used typically for router management purposes. The loopback is always available unless the router is down. It isn't associated with any physical interface. The Layer 2 switches use a VLAN management address for the same purpose.

```
router(config)# interface Loopback0
router(config-if)# ip address [ip address] 255.255.255.255
```

Layer 2 EtherChannel

Etherchannel bundles multiple Ethernet switch ports into a single logical channel for load balancing and bandwidth aggregation. The interface range defines the switch ports to configure. The optional **switchport mode trunk** command will set EtherChannel to trunk multiple VLANs. The channel-group command creates the EtherChannel from the switch ports. The [mode type] keyword assigns the channel setup protocol. PAgP supports auto, desirable and on mode while LACP supports active, passive and on mode.

```
switch# conf t
switch(config)# interface range gigabitethernet0/1-4
switch(config-if-range)# switchport mode access [trunk]
switch(config-if-range)# switchport access vlan [vlan number]
switch(config-if-range)# channel-group [number] mode [pagp | lacp]
switch(config-if-range)# exit
```

Port Channel (Layer 3 EtherChannel)

The Layer 3 port channel is a routed interface on a switch. The initial commands define the port channel with an IP address. That enables it as a routed interface. The second series of commands assigns a switch port interface to the port channel with the channel-group. The channel group number would match the port channel number.

```
switch# conf t
switch(config)# interface port-channel [number]
switch(config)# description [text]
switch(config-if)# no switchport
switch(config-if)# ip address [ip address] [subnet mask]
switch(config-if)# exit
switch(config)# interface [interface slot/port]
switch(config-if-range)# no ip address
switch(config-if-range)# channel-group [number] mode [pagp | lacp]
switch(config-if-range)# exit
```

WAN Serial Interface

The Serial interface is most common for enterprise WAN connectivity. The following are standard commands for configuring a T1 WAN interface.

router(config)# **interface controller t1** [slot/port]
router(config-if)# **clock source [type]**
router(config-if)# **framing** [framing type]
router(config-if)# **linecode** [line encoding]
router(config-if)# **channel-group** [channel-group-number] [timeslots] [range]
router(config)# **interface type** [subinterface number]
router(config-if)# **ip address** [ip address] [subnet mask]

Layer 2 Switching

The standard switching infrastructure is configured with VLANs, inter-switch connectivity and Spanning Tree Protocol features. The following commands enable standard Layer 2 packet forwarding between switches.

Defining VLANs

The following command will create a VLAN on a switch. The VLAN must be created before it is assigned. The VLAN is a foundational feature of switching that defines broadcast domains. Create the VLANs based on company design standards and before configuring switch interfaces.

switch(config)# **vlan** [number]

Switch Access Port

The switch access port is a standard Layer 2 interface typically used for connecting desktops, IP phones, peripherals and wireless access points. The switchport mode access command defines a standard Layer 2 switch port interface. The following series of commands will configure a switch access port with separate access VLAN and voice VLAN. The voice VLAN command allows for assigning two VLANs to an access port. That separates data and voice traffic from the desktop without trunking.

switch(config)# **interface** [interface]
switch(config-if)# **description** [text]
switch(config-if)# **switchport mode access**
switch(config-if)# **switchport access vlan** [number]
switch(config-if)# **switchport voice vlan** [number]

Switch Trunk Port

The trunk is a feature that enables a switch port to forward multiple VLANs across a switch link. There is support for an EtherChannel trunk as well. Unless specified, all VLANs are allowed across the switch trunk link.

```
switch(config)# interface [interface]
switch(config-if)# switchport mode trunk
switch(config-if)# encapsulation dot1q
```

Switch to Router Trunking

The configuration of a trunk between switch and router enables forwarding of traffic from multiple VLAN segments to the WAN. The access ports are defined on the physical switch ports. In addition the subinterfaces are configured on a single router interface. The **switchport trunk native vlan** command best practice assigns a new VLAN instead of the default VLAN 1.

```
switch(config)# interface Gi0/1
switch(config-if)# switchport mode trunk
switch(config-if)# switchport trunk encapsulation dot1q
switch(config-if)# switchport trunk native vlan 255
switch(config-if)# switchport trunk allowed vlan 10,20

router(config)# interface Gi0/0
router(config-if)# no shut
router(config-if)# exit

router(config)# interface Gi0/0.10
router(config-subif)# encapsulation dot1q 10
router(config-subif)# ip address [subinterface ip address] [subnet mask]

router(config-subif)# interface Gi0/0.20
router(config-subif)# encapsulation dot1q 20
router(config-subif)# ip address [subinterface ip address] [subnet mask]
```

Spanning Tree Protocol (STP)

The following commands are used to configure the switch spanning tree mode and enable extended system id feature.

```
switch(config)# spanning-tree mode [pvst rapid-pvst mst]
switch(config)# spanning-tree extend system-id
```

Portfast

The Portfast command is a spanning tree protocol feature deployed to switch access ports. The desktops, peripherals, wireless access points and IP phones do not participate in STP. As a result the Portfast feature allows port forwarding for the assigned access ports.

switch(config)# **interface** [interface]
switch(config-if)# **spanning-tree portfast**

Portfast BPDU Guard

This command is an STP enhancement applied to Portfast enabled switch ports. The access switch port is err-disabled when a BPDU arrives and port is prevented from participating in spanning tree.

switch(config)# **spanning-tree bpdugard enable**

VLAN Trunk Protocol (VTP)

The following commands will configure VTP services on a switch. The VTP domain is created and VTP mode is assigned to the switch.

switch(config)# **vtp domain** [network_group]
switch(config)# **vtp mode** [mode type]
switch(config)# **vtp password** [password]

IP Routing

The following are common IOS commands typical for initial IP routing configuration. The commands are used to define Layer 3 connectivity between routers and multilayer switches. The design requirements would determine the additional device configuration.

Default Gateway

The default-gateway command is used when ip routing is not enabled. The command enables the switch or router to forward packets to a layer 3 device. The IP address of the upstream neighbor router or multilayer switch is specified with the global command.

router(config)# **ip default-gateway** [ip address]

Static Route

The following is the command for configuring a static route. The next hop IP address is used for routing packets to the destination IP address. The administrative distance of static routes are lower than routing protocols. As a result they are the preferred router for the specified destination.

R1(config)# **ip route** [dest. ip address] [subnet mask] [next-hop IP address]

Enhanced Interior Gateway Protocol (EIGRP)

The following commands will enable EIGRP routing. The network command enables EIGRP advertisements on network interfaces assigned to the network address. There is support for one or multiple network commands.

R1(config)# **router eigrp** [autonomous system]
R1(config-router)# **network** [network ip address] [network subnet mask]

Open Shortest Path First (OSPF)

The following command is used to enable OSPF routing. OSPF uses wildcard (reverse dotted notation) for subnet mask. The network commands enable OSPF on router interfaces assigned the network address. In addition the command assigns the OSPF area to the router interface as well.

R1(config)# **router ospf** [process id]
R1(config-router)# **network** [ip address] [wildcard mask] **area** [number]

Border Gateway Protocol (BGP)

The following are standard IOS commands to enable BGP routing. The network command injects the IGP routes from the global routing table into the BGP table. The neighbor command adds the IP address of a remote BGP neighbor (peer) to the BGP routing table.

R1(config)# **router bgp** [as number]
R1(config-router)# **network** [network-number] **mask** [network-mask]
R1(config-router)# **neighbor** [ip-address] **remote-as** [as number]

Hot Standby Router Protocol (HSRP)

HSRP group is a standby group defined with at least 2 routers. The active router is configured with a higher priority than the standby router. The multicast address 224.0.0.102 is used to send HSRP version 2 hello messages. The IP address assigned to the HSRP group is configured on both group members with the **standby ip** command.

```
R1(config)# interface [interface]
R1(config-if)# ip address [ip address] [subnet mask]
R1(config-if)# standby version 2
R1(config-if)# standby 10 preempt
R1(config-if)# standby 10 priority 110
R1(config-if)# standby 10 ip [standby ip address]


R2(config)# interface [interface]
R2(config-if)# ip address [ip address] [subnet mask]
R2(config-if)# standby version 2
R2(config-if)# standby 10 preempt
R2(config-if)# standby 10 priority 100
R2(config-if)# standby 10 ip [standby ip address]
```

Access Security

The following commands provide standard security for access to switches and routers. There is minimal network security with devices that are using the default Cisco security settings. Consider the company security policies and configure the network devices accordingly.

Username

The username command configures designated users and assigns the security level for access to the device.

```
router(config)# username admin privilege [15] secret [5]
```

Enable Password

This command will setup an enable password with assigned security level for accessing the device. The password is unencrypted (text) with the running configuration script.

```
router(config)# enable password [level] [password]
```

Service Password-Encryption

This command will provide a mild encryption to the enable password in the running configuration script for added security.

```
router(config)# service password-encryption
```

Enable Secret

This command will setup an enable password with MD5 hashing for optimized security. The enable secret provides stronger password security for switches and routers than service password-encryption.

router(config)# **enable secret level** [level] [password]

TACACS+ Server

The following are standard AAA commands for enabling TACACS+ server based security access to switches and routers.

R1(config)# **aaa new-model**
R1(config)# **aaa session-id common**
R1(config)# **tacacs-server host** [ip address]
R1(config)# **aaa authentication login default group tacacs+ local**
R1(config)# **aaa authentication enable default group tacacs+ enable**
R1(config)# **aaa authentication ppp default local**
R1(config)# **aaa accounting exec default action-type start-stop group tacacs+**
R1(config)# **aaa accounting commands 15 default action-type start-stop group tacacs+**

Port Security

The purpose of port security is to limit traffic to a switch port for security purposes. The **port-security maximum** [number] defines the maximum number of secure MAC addresses that can be assigned to the switch port. In addition a single MAC address is assignable to the switch port.

switch(config)# **switchport port-security**
switch(config)# **switchport port-security maximum** [number]
switch(config)# **switchport port-security aging time** [time sec]
switch(config)# **switchport port-security violation restrict**
switch(config)# **switchport port-security aging type inactivity**

HTTP Secure Server

Cisco allows for management of their network devices with a web browser interface. An example is Web-Based Device Manager available with IOS .tar files for configuring routers and switches. The following commands disable the default http server and enables secure server with support for SSLv3. The web browser encrypts the connection between desktop and network device for optimized security.

router(config)# **no ip http server**
router(config)# **ip http secure-server**

IOS Troubleshooting

The boot (startup) procedure describes the sequence of events when powering on a switch or router. It is a key aspect of troubleshooting IOS problems. The device goes through a check to verify all hardware first. The boot loader starts the bootstrap program and reads the configuration register. The settings for the configuration register affect how the startup configuration script and where IOS image are loaded. The device boots to ROMmon mode if there no IOS image detected.

Figure 3-3 Cisco Boot Startup Sequence for Switches and Routers

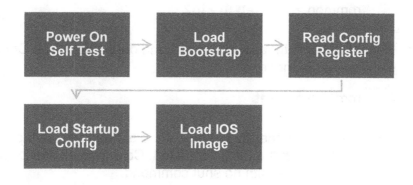

Configuration Register Settings

The Cisco routers have a configuration register that allows network engineers to manage the boot process. The following describes the standard register settings and effect.

0x2100 = boot into ROMmon mode and don't load any IOS.

0x2101 = load the first listed IOS from flash and ignore system boot command from the startup configuration file.

0x2102 = (default setting) load IOS image specified with boot system command from the startup configuration. The first IOS listed in Flash is loaded when there is no boot system configured

0x2142 = ignore the startup configuration in NVRAM and boot first IOS image listed in flash (for password recovery)

Router Password Recovery

The procedure for doing a password recovery is based on the hardware platform. There is a standard procedure for doing password recovery on routers that support IOS 12.0 and 15.0 release versions.

Step 1: Boot router to start ROMmon mode with Ctrl-Break or Ctrl-C.

rommon >

Step 2: Modify configuration register with confreg 0x2142 to prevent the startup configuration script from loading. The password is configured with the configuration file.

rommon > **confreg 0x2142**

Step 3: Reboot router with reset command and during boot type Ctrl-C to exit from setup mode.

rommon > **reset**

Step 4: From the Exec mode prompt type enable. Load the startup configuration with the copy command. Configure all previously enabled interfaces with no shut command.

router > **enable**
router# **copy startup-config running-config**

Step 5: From the Exec mode prompt type enable.

router > **enable**
router# **enable secret** [level] [new password]

Step 6: Modify the configuration register with confreg 0x2102, save changes to the startup configuration and reboot router.

router# **confreg 0x2102**
router# **write mem**
router# **reload**

Catalyst Switch Password Recovery

The following is a step by step procedure for doing a password recovery on the Catalyst 2960, 3550, 3560 and 3750 switches. It includes commands for unstacked and stacked configuration.

Step 1: Power off the unstacked switch or switch stack members and Restart the master switch

Step 2: Press and hold the mode button located on the left side of the front panel and power on switch. Based on the Cisco Catalyst switch model do one of the following:

Catalyst 2960:   Release the Mode button when the SYST LED flashes amber and then turns solid green. When the Mode button is released the SYST LED flashes green

Catalyst 3550:   Release the Mode button when the LED above Port1x goes off.

Catalyst 3560:   Release the Mode button after 15 seconds when the SYST LED turns solid green. When the Mode button is released, the SYST LED flashes green.

Catalyst 3750:   Release the Mode button after 15 seconds when the SYST LED turns solid green. When the Mode button is released, the SYST LED flashes green.

Step 3: The switch will boot to the switch: prompt where the following commands are entered. The flash_init command initializes the flash file system. The loadhelper command is used for loading helper files to memory.

> switch: **flash_init**
> switch: **loadhelper**

Step 4: Run the dir flash: command to verify the config.text filename where the switch configuration is stored. From the switch: prompt issue the following command.

> switch: **rename flash:config.text flash:config.text.old**

Step 5: Reboot the switch with the following command.

> switch: **boot**

Step 6: Answer **No** to the prompt after the switch reboots.
You are prompted to start the setup program. Enter N at the prompt: Continue with the configuration dialog? [yes/no]: **N**

Step 7: Enter Privileged Exec mode from User Exec mode with the enable command. Enter global configuration mode and rename the configuration file to its original name:

> switch> **enable**
> switch# **conf t**
> switch(config)# **rename flash:config.text.old flash:config.text**
> switch(config)# **exit**
> switch#

Note: At this point for a switch stack password recovery, power on the connected stack members and wait until the stack members have initialized. The unstacked switch is not rebooted.

Step 8: Copy the switch configuration file to memory with the following command and hit enter to verify

> switch# **copy flash:config.text system:running-config**
> Source filename [config.text]?
> Destination filename [running-config]?

Step 9: Enter global configuration mode and change the enable password. the secret password can be from 1 to 25 alphanumeric characters, can start with a number, case sensitive, permits spaces and ignores leading spaces.

> switch# **conf t**
> switch (config)# **enable secret** [password]
> switch (config)# **exit**
> switch#

Step 10: Save the new password to the startup configuration with the following command. Re-enable the SVI interface with no shut command.

> switch# **write mem**

112

Step 11: Reload the 3560X or 3750X switch with the standard reload command from global configuration mode.

> switch# **reload**
> Proceed with reload? [confirm] **y**

> For a stacked configuration, reload the 3750X switch stack master with the following command:

> switch# **reload slot** [stack-master-member-number]
> Proceed with reload? [confirm] **y**

Corrupt IOS Image

The switch or router boots to ROMmon mode when there is a problem with loading the IOS software image. The typical causes include corrupt IOS image, corrupt Flash memory or deleted IOS image. The following describe password recovery for Cisco ISR series routers and Catalyst switches.

Cisco ISR Series Routers

The USB is the fastest and easiest method for replacing the corrupted IOS image. There is the option as well to copy over a newer IOS to router Flash and edit (point) the boot system flash command for that image.

Step 1: Power on the router and while it starts, press the Ctrl-Break key to enter ROMmon mode.

Step 2: Format the USB flash drive with FAT16 file system. That formats USB for compatibility with Cisco USB slot and decreases USB to 1 GB size. IOS 15.1 release supports FAT32 for larger USB drives.

> rommon > **format usbflash0:**

Step 3: Copy the required IOS release version to USB flash drive. The IOS filename must match unless the IOS is being upgraded.

> **copy** directory\[IOS filename] **usbflash0:**

Step 4: While the router is powered off, plug in the USB flash drive to the USB port on the router.

Step 5: Power on the router and while it starts, press the Ctrl-Break key to enter ROMmon mode.

Step 6: From the ROMmon mode prompt enter the following command to copy over the IOS image from USB drive to router Flash.

> rommon > **copy usbflash0:**[IOS filename] **flash:**
> rommon > **reset**

Tech Note: There is the option to boot IOS from USB flash drive as well. The current IOS release versions support that feature however it will require upgrade for some older IOS 12.x code. Upgrade the bootstrap loader to 12.4(13r)T11 or later with the recommended IOS version from Cisco Feature Navigator. Copy the IOS (bin file) to a supported USB thumb drive. From ROMmon mode prompt (or switch: prompt) type the following command:

> *rommon > **boot system usbflash0:**[IOS filename]*
> *switch: **boot usbflash0:**[IOS filename]*

Cisco Catalyst Switches

The following procedure for replacing a corrupt IOS image applies to the Catalyst 2960, 3550, 3560 and 3750 series switches. The easiest method is the USB flash drive available with Cisco access switches.

Step 1: Press and hold the mode button located on the left side of the front panel and power on switch. Based on the Cisco Catalyst switch model do one of the following:

Catalyst 2960: Release the Mode button when the SYST LED flashes amber and then turns solid green. When the Mode button is released the SYST LED flashes green

Catalyst 3550: Release the Mode button when the LED above Port1x goes off.

Catalyst 3560: Release the Mode button after 15 seconds when the SYST LED turns solid green. When the Mode button is released, the SYST LED flashes green.

Catalyst 3750: Release the Mode button after 15 seconds when the SYST LED turns solid green. When the Mode button is released, the SYST LED flashes green.

Step 2: That starts the switch in ROMmon mode. From the ROMmon prompt format USB flash drive for FAT16 compatibility.

switch: **format usbflash0**:

Step 3: Copy the required IOS release version to USB flash drive. The IOS filename must match unless the IOS is being upgraded.

copy directory\[IOS filename] **usbflash0:**

Step 4: Plug in the USB flash drive to the switch USB slot

Step 5: Reinitialize the switch Flash memory with the following command.

switch: **flash_init**

Step 6: Replace the corrupt IOS file with the following copy command.

switch: **copy usbflash0:**[IOS filename] **flash:** [IOS filename]
switch: **reset**

Step 7: (Option) Edit boot flash command and point to an upgraded IOS fil

switch# **conf t**
switch(config)# **boot flash:**[/IOS filename]
switch# **wr mem**
switch# **reload**

Cisco Catalyst Switches (.tar file)

Cisco IOS images file types are available in .bin and .tar file format. The Cisco IOS .bin file images are stored in the compressed tar file. Extract the bin file from the tar file with any zip program that can read a .tar file. The following describes the procedure for replacing a corrupt IOS image based on the IOS tar file image. The following example copies the file from a TFTP server however the USB Flash method is available as well.

Step 1: Download the .tar file and unzip/extract the IOS .bin file.

Step 2: Copy the .bin file to switch Flash to replace the current .bin file.

switch: **copy tftp: flash:**

Step 3: Reload the switch

switch: **reset**

Chapter 4

IOS Show Commands

Overview

There are hundreds of IOS show commands available for managing and troubleshooting network devices. The following is a list of 180+ standard IOS show commands for the following hardware platforms. The show commands are supported from the global configuration mode prompt.

1. Switches and Routers (Common)
2. Cisco Routers
3. Catalyst Access Switches
4. Catalyst 4500 and 6500 Switches
5. Nexus 5000 and 7000 Switches
6. Nexus 1000V for VMware Switch
7. Wireless LAN Controllers
8. ASA 5500 Firewalls
9. WAAS Devices

Cisco Switches and Routers (Common)

The following show commands are common to Cisco Catalyst switches and routers that support standard IOS platform software. The command line include optional [bracket] arguments.

- Show IOS Code, Licenses and Hardware: **# show version**

- Show Connected Devices: **# show cdp neighbor [detail]**

- List IP Routes: **# show ip route [static] [ospf] [eigrp] [bgp]**

- Interface Details: **# show interface [*interface*] [summary]**

- Show Connect Status of Interfaces: **# show ip interface brief**

- Show Port Channels: **# show interface port-channel [1-64]**

- Show Chassis and Module Serial Number: **# show inventory**

- List All Files on Flash: **# show flash:**

- Support File for Cisco TAC: **# show tech-support**

- Show the Running Configuration: **# show running-config**

- Show the Start Configuration: **# show startup-config**

- List ARP Table Entries: **# show ip arp**

- Show DTP Status Per Interface: **# show dtp [interface]**

- Power Supply, Fan, Temperature: **# show environment all**

- Etherchannel Interfaces: **# show etherchannel summary**

- Show System Message Log: **# show logging**

- Show CPU Utilization: **# show processes cpu [history]**

- Show IP SLA Status: **# show ip sla responder**

- NTP Server: **# show ntp status**

- PagP Links: **# show pagp [counter] [neighbor] [internal]**

- Show Interface Status, IP Addressing: **# show protocols**

- Show VTP Configuration: **# show vtp status**

- Show Policy-Maps: **# show policy-map [name] [interface]**

Cisco Routers

The following show commands are applicable to only Cisco routers that support standard IOS platform software.

- Show Enabled License Features: **# show license feature**

- NHRP Cache: **# show ip nhrp summary [detail] [brief]**

- NHRP Registration Status: **# show ip nhrp nhs detail**

- Show HSRP Information : **# show standby all**

- List All Configured VLANs: **# show vlans**

- List Total, Free, Used Memory: **# show memory statistics**

- Show Layer 1 Serial Interface Status: **# show controllers t1**

- List Connected EIGRP Peers: **# show ip eigrp neighbors**

- Show EIGRP Interfaces: **# show ip eigrp interfaces**

- Show EIGRP Topology Table: **# show ip eigrp topology**

- Connected OSPF Neighbors: **# show ip ospf neighbor**

- Show OSPF Interface Details: **# show ip ospf interface**

- Show OSPF Database: **# show ip ospf database**

- Show Status of IKE Connection: **# show crytpo isakmp sa**

- Show Status of IPsec Connection: **# show crypto ipsec sa**

- Show All Active VoIP Calls: **# show call active voice**

- CEF Switching: **# show cef state**

- Netflow: **# show ip flow [interface] [export] [top-talkers]**

- Show VoIP SCCP Status: **# show sccp**

- Show Configured Data Trunks: **# show trunk group**
- Show WCCP Details: **# show wccp [all]**
- Show WAAS Details: **# show waas status**

Cisco Catalyst Access Switches

The following show commands are applicable to Cisco access switches that support standard IOS platform software.

- LACP Status: **# show lacp [1-128] [neigh] [int] [counter]**
- Summarize STP Status: **# show spanning-tree summary**
- Show Boot File Used: **# show boot**
- List CAM Table Entries: **# show mac address-table**
- Show Stack Ring Details: **# show switch detail [neighbors]**
- Show Terminal Line Usage: **# show users**
- Show Configured VLANs: **# show vlan**
- Show Memory Usage: **# show memory**
- Show Port Status, VLAN, Duplex, Speed, Transceiver:

   # show interface status
- All Etherchannel Groups: **# show etherchannel summary**
- Show Etherchannel Group: **# show etherchannel [1-128]**

Cisco Catalyst 4500 and 6500 Switches

The following show commands are applicable to Cisco 4500 and 6500 distribution switches that support IOS software. The Catalyst 4500 series switches run IOS-XE and Catalyst 6500 series switches use standard IOS.

- Show Port Status, VLAN, Duplex, Speed, Transceiver:

   # show interface status
- Show Port Channel: **# show interface port-channel [1-128]**
- Line Cards, Sup Engine, MAC Address: **# show module**
- List All Files on Boot Flash: **# show bootflash:**
- Show Total, Free, Used Memory: **# show memory statistics**
- Show HSRP Details (6500): **# show hsrp brief**
- Show HSRP Details (4500): **# show standby all**

- Supervisor Engine Redundancy Status: **# show redundancy status**
- Show VSS Redundancy **# show switch virtual redundancy**
- Show VSS Information: **# show switch virtual**
- Show VSS Peer Link Status: **# show switch virtual link**
- Show UDLD Status Per Interface: **# show udld port**

Cisco Nexus 5000 and 7000 Switches

The following show commands are applicable to Cisco Nexus switches supporting NX-OS software.

- List All Configured Features and Status: **# show feature**
- Show Feature-Set Status: **# show feature-set**
- Show Status of Connected Fabric Extender: **# show fex**
- Show VPC Configuration: **# show vpc**
- Show Licenses Enabled: **# show license usage**
- Show Port Channel Details: **# show port-channel summary**
- Show Interface Status, Duplex, Speed, VLAN, Transceiver:

    # show interface status
- Show Supervisor Engine Redundancy Status: (7000)

    # show system redundancy status
- Summarize HSRP Configuration (7000): **# show hsrp**
- Show Interfaces Assigned to VDC: **# show vdc membership**
- Show Details for Any Ethernet Interface:

    # show interface ethernet [*interface*]
- Show Load Sharing Configuration: **# show ip load-sharing**
- VPC Peer Keepalive Link Status: **# show vpc keep-alive**
- Show IP Traffic Statistics: **# show ip traffic**
- Show Interface Hardware: **# show interface capabilities**
- Show CPU and Memory Usage: **# show system resources**
- Show Power, Fan and Temperature: **# show environment**

Cisco Nexus 1000V Switch

The following show commands are applicable to Cisco Nexus 1000V switch for VMware and NX-OS software.

- Port Profiles: **# show port-profile name [*profile name*]**
- VSM vCenter Server Connection: **# show svs connections**
- Show vEth Interface: **# show interface vethernet [*interface*]**
- vEth Trunk: **# show interface vethernet [*interface*] [trunk]**
- Show All Virtual Interfaces **# show interface virtual**
- Show Management Interface **# show interface mgmt 0**
- Password Strength: **# show password strength-check**
- Active Connections: **# show svs connections [conn_name]**
- VSM Domain Configuration: **# show svs domain**
- Show All SVS Neighbors: **# show svs neighbors**
- Software Release Level: **# show system vem feature level**
- Show System Image File Running: **# show boot**
- VSD and Port Profiles: **# show virtual-service-domain brief**

Cisco Wireless LAN Controllers (WLC)

The following show commands are applicable to Cisco Wireless LAN Controller (WLC) software.

- Show Code Version, Licenses, AP Support: **# show sysinfo**
- Show AP Configuration: **# show ap config general [*ap*]**
- Show WLANs on Controller: **# show wlan summary**
- List ARP table: **# show arp switch**
- Show CPU Utilization: **# show cpu**
- Show Serial Number, Crypto Accelerator **# show inventory**
- Show WLC Licenses **# show license summary**
- Show Network Configuration: **# show network summary**
- Show QoS: **# show qos [bronze] [gold] [platinum] [silver]**
- Show Summary of Active Clients: **# show client summary**
- Show DHCP Information: **# show dhcp summary**

- Channel Auto Setup # **show advanced 802.11 [*a b*] channel**

- AP RF Summary # **show advanced 802.11 [*a b*] summary**

- Show WPS Summary Information: # **show wps summary**

- Summary of System Interfaces: # **show interface summary**

- Show System Interface Details # **show interface detailed**

- Show WLC Port Settings: # **show port summary**

- Port Details: # **show stats port detailed [*port number*]**

Cisco ASA 5500 Firewall

The following show commands are applicable to Cisco ASA 5500-X firewalls supporting ASA software.

- Show ASA Code, Licenses, Serial Numbers, Memory, Modules, Uptime,

  MAC Address:# **show version**

- Show Running Configuration: # **show running-config**

- Show Syslog Settings and Messages Log: # **show logging**

- Show Configured VLANs: # **show vlan**

- Show All Interface Details: # **show interface detail**

- Show ARP Table: # **show arp**

- Show Cluster Members: # **show cluster [info] [conn]**

- Show Connection Information:

  # **show conn address [*ip address*] [detail]**

- Show Number of Connection: # **show conn count**

- Show Start-Up Configuration: # **show configuration**

- Show CPU Utilization: # **show cpu [detail]**

- Show IKE Connectivity**: # show crypto isakmp sa**

- Show IPsec Connectivity: # **show crypto ipsec sa**

- Show IKEv1 SA Details: # **show crypto ikev1 sa detail**

- Show IKEv2 SA Details: # **show crypto ikev2 sa detail**

- Show Power, Fan, Temperature: # **show environment**

- Show Firewall Mode: # **show firewall**

- Show IPS Information: # **show ips**

- Show All Interfaces: **# show interface**
- Show Redundancy Status and Configuration: **# show failover**
- Show Files on Flash (Code etc.): **# show flash0:**
- Show Chassis Serial Number and PID: **# show inventory**
- Show Total, Free, Used Memory: **# show memory [detail]**
- Show Security Context: **# show mode**
- Show Modules, MAC Address, ASA Code: **# show module**
- Show NAT Policies and Counters: **# show nat [detail]**
- Show Password Encryption Settings:

  # show password encryption
- Show Various Performance Metrics: **# show perfmon**
- Show CPU Utilization: **# show proc cpu-usage [cpu-hog]**
- Show Memory Utilization Detail: **# show processes memory**
- Show Firewall Route Table: **# show route**
- Show Packet Rate and Drops Per Interface: **# show traffic**
- Show Configured VLANs: **# show vlan**
- Show NAT Translation Table: **# show xlate**

Cisco WAAS

The following show commands are applicable to Cisco WAAS hardware platforms running WAAS software.

- Show WAAS Code Version: **# show version**
- CIFS Optimization Information: **# show cifs**
- Show DRE Configuration: **# show dre**
- WAAS Interception Method: **# show interception-method**
- Show Memory Blocks and Statistics: **# show memory**
- Current WAAS Device Mode: **# show device-mode current**
- Show Virtual Blade Information: **# show virtual-blade**
- Show CPU and Memory Usage: **# top**
- Network Diagnostic Tests: **# test self-diagnostic all**
- Show Syslog Settings and Messages Log: **# show logging**

- Show WAAS Route Table: **# show ip routes**
- Show License Status: **# show license**
- Show Accelerator Status: **# show accelerator**
- Show TCP Connections: **# show statistics connection**
- Show TFO Statistics: **# show statistics tfo [detail]**
- Show Configuration for Interfaces: **# show interface**
- Show WCCP services: **# show wccp services**
- Show WCCP status: **# show wccp status**
- Show GRE Packet Counters: **# show wccp gre**
- Show All WCCP Enabled Routers: **# show wccp routers**
- Show All WAE Engines: **# show wccp wide-area-engine**

Router / Switch IOS Commands:

- Show WAAS Packet Redirection: **# show ip wccp**
- Show WCCP Interfaces: **# show ip wccp interfaces detail**
- Show WCCP Status: **# show ip wccp all [summary]**
- WAAS Disk Usage: **# show disks details**
- Users With Admin Privileges: **# show users administrative**

Show Help Commands

- Device> **enable**
- Device# **?**
- Device# **show ?**
- Device# **show** [command] **?**
- Device# **show run** [string]
- Device# **show debug ?**
- Device# **dir /all**
- Device# **show memory scan**

Third Party Tools

The following describe some standard tools available for network testing and troubleshooting. Some of the tools enable network engineers to verify network design, configuration and IOS upgrades before deployment.

Ping

The use of ping is standard for testing round trip time network latency. In addition it will report on packet loss between source and destination. The ping uses ICMP echo messages packets to send between source and destination. The following command tests network latency from where the command was issued to an ip address (server or network device). The –t sends continuous pings until ctrl-break. The –a returns the device name while –l increases packet size to maximum 1500 bytes. The –r flag provides traceroute information for hops between source and destination. The second ping example allows prompt based selection of command arguments.

router# **ping** -t -a –r –l 1500 [ip address]

router# **ping**

> router# ping
>
> Protocol [ip]:
>
> Target IP address:
>
> Repeat count [5]:
>
> Datagram size [100]:
>
> Timeout in seconds [2]:
>
> Extended commands [n]:
>
> Source address or interface:
>
> Type of service [0]:
>
> Set DF bit in IP header? [no]:
>
> Validate reply data? [no]:
>
> Data pattern [0xABCD]:
>
> Loose, Strict, Record, Timestamp, Verbose [none]:
>
> Sweep range of sizes [n]:

Traceroute

The network engineer will use traceroute to analyze hop by hop packet routing between source and destination. It is an effective tool that identifies problems with suboptimal routing. In addition it is used for understanding network design and topology. There is a Layer 2 traceroute available from Cisco as well that will trace layer 2 switch topology at a data center for instance. That will require CDP enabled at all switches. The WinMTR tool combines ping and traceroute features to examine network latency and packet loss per router hop.

router# **traceroute** [ip address]

> Protocol [ip]:
>
> Target IP address:
>
> Source address:
>
> DSCP Value [0]: ! Only displayed if a topology is configured.
>
> Numeric display [n]:
>
> Timeout in seconds [3]:
>
> Probe count [3]:
>
> Minimum Time to Live [1]:
>
> Maximum Time to Live [30]:
>
> Port Number [33434]:
>
> Loose, Strict, Record, Timestamp, Verbose [none]:

Virtual Internet Routing Lab (VIRL)

Cisco's Virtual Internet Routing Lab (VIRL) is a network simulation tool with a GUI for proof of concept testing. The OpenStack backend includes virtual versions of multiple software platforms. That would include IOS, IOS XR, NX-OS and ASA firewall. The software images run on the hypervisor and support 10 IOS or IOS XE instances that are connected with a defined topology to a single vSwitch. The simulation tool allows network engineers to define the network topology connecting multiple virtual routers, switches and servers. The platform translates the virtual machines running actual Cisco IOS software platforms. The network design model enables validation of configuration scripts, failover testing and to verify new feature behavior. It is an effective tool for learning the IOS platform before deployment as well. New IOS upgrades can be verified with the virtual lab to work and fixing bugs where applicable.

Network disruptions are minimized with testing before any maintenance window as well. There is a personal edition (virl.cisco.com) deployed to the company network or a hosted version available through Cisco DEVNET.

Multiserver Network Simulator

The advantage of Multiserver Network Simulator is to create a virtual network for testing purposes. The Windows based tool allows the network engineer or application developer to specify multiple servers and switches. The network test bed design is limited by the number of available IP addresses and TCP ports available. In addition server hardware will limit the network size as well. The following include the virtual device types.

- Network switches (8, 100 and 1000 ports)
- SNMP based switches
- HTTP server
- FTP server
- SMTP server
- DNS server
- Basic server (open TCP port for incoming requests)

For instance the network engineer can setup a network test bed with 200 servers and 10 switches in minutes. The program will auto discover all available IP addresses on the local machine. The network engineer selects an IP address and protocol to add a virtual server. From there the server is configured and added to the network.

- SNMP enabled switch with traffic counters per switch port.
- Web server request/response traffic.
- Simulate FTP server login requests and file download.
- SMTP server that accepts protocol connections with authentication.
- DNS server requests for the DNS name.

SoftPerfect WAN Emulator

The SCE WAN emulator is available to network engineers and application developers for network and application testing. The Windows based emulator supports multiple throughput (bandwidth) latency and packet loss settings. That would simulate a variety of network conditions and verify performance. There are profiles for multiple WAN protocols that include broadband services. The network connectivity tests are based on path characteristics from source to destination. That would include switches, routers, firewalls and WAAS devices. The application testing considers Layer 7 performance for individual transactions. The application response time based on varying latency and throughput is confirmed. The additional WAN emulators available include WANEM (Linux) and Shunra.

SolarWinds WAN Killer

SolarWinds provides a load testing tool available with the engineer toolkit. The purpose of the traffic generator is verify network design and equipment capacity testing. That would include network capacity, load balancing and device configuration. The TCP/UDP random packets are sent between a source and destination path. The network engineer can vary circuit bandwidth, load percent and packet size for each test profile. In addition there is feature set support for adjusting network latency and QoS priority setting. Load balancing behavior is confirmed with WAN killer as well.

CCNA Quiz

The command line [brackets] denote additional typed commands that vary. That would include specific interface, VLAN number or optional command line argument for instance.

OSI Model

1. Name the 7 layers of the OSI model ?

   Answer:

   Physical, Data Link, Network, Transport, Session, Presentation, Application

2. What layer is routing ?

   Answer: Network

3. What layer is switching ?

   Answer: Data Link

4. What layer is TCP protocol ?

   Answer: Transport

5. What are the layers of the TCP/IP model ?

   Answer:

   The newer TCP/IP model is similar to the OSI model. The 4 layers include network, internet, transport and application.

6. Describe the purpose of each OSI Layer ?

   Answer:

   - The Application Layer - services to network applications.
   - The Presentation Layer - data translation and encoding.
   - Session Layer - session setup for data and tear down.
   - Transport Layer – client to server connection flow control and error retransmission.
   - Network Layer - routing with IP addressing and best path selection.
   - Data Link - layer 2 connectivity based on MAC address and media contention.
   - Physical Layer - putting data on the physical media as bits.

7. What layer is DNS with the newer TCP model ?

   Answer: Application

8. What is data encapsulation ?

   Answer:

   This is the process whereby each OSI layer adds a header (encapsulation) in front of the data from an upper layer. The header is comprised of control information. The PDU is the name commonly given to the header and data.

9. Define unicasts, multicasts and broadcasts ?

   Answer:

   - Unicasts - packets sent from a single source to a single destination.
   - Multicasts - packets sent from a single source to multiple destinations.
   - Broadcasts - packets sent from a single source to all destinations on a network

10. Name the 3 layers of the Cisco multilayer design model ?

    Answer: Access, Distribution, Core

Cisco Basic Router Configuration

11. What commands for global configuration mode ?

    Answer:

    router# **conf t**

12. How do you configure a hostname ?

    Answer:

    router(config)# **hostname** [name]

13. How do you configure a banner notice ?

    Answer:

    router(config)# **banner motd #**

14. What command encrypts the enable password in the configuration ?

    Answer:

    router(config)# **service password-encryption**

15. How do you setup an enable password with optimized encryption ?

    Answer:

    router(config)# **enable secret level** [level] [password]

16. How do you configure all VTY lines with a password ?

    Answer:

    router(config)# **line vty 0 4**
    router(config-line)# **password cisco**
    router(config-line)# **login**

17. How do you configure a default DNS domain name for router ?

    Answer:

    router(config)# **ip domain-name** [companydomainname.com]

18. How do you configure SSH with 2048 bit size ?

    Answer:

    R1(config)# **crypto key generate rsa general-keys modulus 2048**
    R1{config-line)# **transport input ssh telnet**

19. How do you configure a layer 3 interface ?

    Answer:

    router(config)# **interface** [interface]
    router(config-if)# **description** [text string]
    router(config-if)# **ip address** [ip address] [subnet mask]

20. What command is used to configure a DNS name server ?

    Answer:

    switch(config)# **ip name-server** [ip address]

21. How do you list the running configuration on a router ?

    Answer:

    router# **show running-config**

22. How do you list the IOS code version on a router ?

    Answer:

    router# **show version**

23. How do you list the interface connection status and errors ?

Answer:

router# **show interface** [interface]

24. What commands are used to configure a DHCP pool on a router ?

Answer:

router(config)# **ip dhcp pool** [name]
router(config)# **network** [ip address]
router(dhcp-config)# **dns-server** [ip address]
router(dhcp-config)# **default-router** [ip address]

25. What is the command to copy IOS code to flash memory ?

Answer:

router# **copy tftp: flash:**

26. Command to list ip address and connection status for all interfaces ?

Answer:

router# **show ip interface brief**

27. What command is used to show all connected neighbors ?

Answer:

router# **show cdp neighbor** [detail]

28. How do you copy the running configuration to startup configuration ?

Answer:

router# **copy running-config startup-config**
router# **write mem** (alternate)

29. What command will list the directory on flash ?

Answer:

router# **dir /all**

30. What command assigns an IOS filename from flash for bootup ?

Answer:

router(config)# **boot system flash flash:** [filename]

31. What command will delete a file from flash memory ?

   Answer:

   router# **delete flash:[filename]**

32. What command will delete the startup-config ?

   Answer:

   router# **erase startup-config**

Routing

33. Define static routing ?

   Answer:

   Adds a route to the global routing table. The packets are forwarded from a specific subnet to a specific remote subnet.

34. What is the purpose of a default route ?

   Answer:

   All packets from all local subnets are forwarded to the network route defined with the default route command.

35. What is a dynamic route ?

   Answer:

   Routes advertised by routing protocols and added to the global routing table based on best path selection.

36. What is Administrative Distance (AD) ?

   Answer:

   It is a static value based on the routing protocol and used by the router to determine what route is installed in the global routing table. The AD and metrics are used to select the routes installed into the routing table only. The longest match rule determines what route is selected when there are multiple routes to the same destination.

37. What is the command for configuring a static route ?

   Answer:

   router# **ip route** [dest. ip address] [subnet] [next-hop ip address]

38. What is the AD for static, EIGRP and OSPF routes ?

Answer: (Administrative Distance)

Static Route = 1
EIGRP = 90
OSPF = 110

39. Define SVI and how is it configured on a Catalyst switch ?

Answer:

The SVI is a layer 3 interface configured on a switch for VLAN routing and as the VLAN default gateway.

router(config)# **ip routing**
router(config)# **interface vlan** [number]
router(config-if)# **ip address** [ip address] [subnet mask]

40. What happens to MAC address of a packet across multiple hops ?

Answer:

The source and destination MAC address for the packet (data link frame) is stripped off with each hop. The network device (hop) rewrites the source MAC address for packet with its MAC address. The destination MAC address for the packet is changed as well to the next hop MAC address. That is obtained from the ARP table or a new ARP if not in ARP table. The source and destination IP address for each packet per session does not change.

41. What is the purpose of the IP header TTL field ?

Answer:

It is a field with IP header that decrements each time a packet traverses a router. That prevents routing loops as packet is dropped after decrementing to zero. The default value for the TTL count in the IP header is 255.

42. How does Split Horizon work ?

Answer:

Prevents routing loops by imposing the rule that states a route learned from an interface cannot be advertised to that interface. It is the default for RIP, EIGRP and IGRP.

43. What is the purpose of route poisoning ?

Answer:

It increases the hop count so it is larger than the maximum hop count. That is advertised to neighbor routers where the route is declared unreachable. The receiving router advertises the same route to the source router as well.

44. What is the EIGRP holddown timer ?

Answer:

It is the amount of time equal to 3 hello packets the EIGRP router waits before declaring the neighbor unreachable. The holddown timer starts when a hello packet is not sent from an EIGRP neighbor.

45. What is a distance vector routing protocol and name 2 examples ?

Answer:

The distance vector routing protocol uses distance (number of hops) to determine route cost and best path selection. Examples include IGRP and RIP.

46. What is the advantage of link state routing and name an example ?

Answer: Faster convergence and less bandwidth usage for updates. An example is OSPF.

47. What is the command to enable OSPF routing ?

Answer:

OSPF uses wildcard (reverse dotted notation) for the subnet mask.

router# **router ospf** [process id]
router# **network** [ip address] [wildcard mask] **area** [number]

48. What metric does OSPF use and how is that calculated ?

Answer:

Note: The link bandwidth is referenced from bandwidth command
cost = 100 Mbps / link bandwidth

49. What is the common backbone area for OSPF ?

Answer: Area 0

50. What is the purpose of an OSPF designated router (DR) ?

Answer:

The DR is used for deploying OSPF to a multi-access network type such as Ethernet. The DR is the hub for advertising routes to multiple OSPF neighbor routers (spokes). The purpose of the DR is to minimize routing advertisements. The DR sends routing updates to multicast 224.0.0.6 address. The router with the highest priority and router ID is elected as DR.

51. What is the difference between standard and extended access lists ?

Answer:

The standard access list use a default range from 1-99 to the list and filters traffic based on source IP address only. The extended access lists start at 100 and can filter on source IP address, destination IP address, applications ports etc.

Cisco Switch Configuration

52. Define a collision domain on a switch ?

Answer: The switch creates a separate collision domain per port.

53. Define a broadcast domain ?

Answer: VLAN creates a separate broadcast domain on a switch for assigned port/s.

54. Name the private RFC 1918 IP addressing ?

Answer:

10.0.0.0 - 10.255.255.255 = 10.0.0.0 /8
172.16.0.0 - 172.31.255.255 = 172.16.0.0 /12
192.168.0.0 - 192.168.255.255 = 192.168.0.0 /16

55. Define switch CAM table and command to list the entries ?

Answer:

The CAM table populates MAC addresses with associated switch ports and VLAN membership. The command to list the CAM table is **show mac address-table**

56. What is an ARP table and the command to list entries ?

Answer:

The ARP table is associated with layer 3 enabled devices. Each entry for devices is comprised of IP address, MAC address and VLAN assignment.

57. What is the purpose of VLANs ?

Answer:

The VLAN assigns one or more switch ports to the same broadcast domain.

58. What is full duplex ?

Answer:

The full duplex enabled link sends and receives data across an Ethernet or WAN link simultaneously. The ports that support full duplex create two separate collision domains.

59. Describe how CSMA/CD works ?

Answer:

- Desktop that has a frame to send listens until Ethernet segment (VLAN) is not busy.
- When network segment is not busy, desktop starts sending packet.
- The desktop verifies no collision and signals all neighbor if there is a collision.
- The collision causes each desktop on that VLAN to start a random timer and wait before resending the packet.

60. Name the OSI layer for MAC address and the two components ?

Answer:

The MAC address is layer 2 (data link layer) and comprised of a 24-bit manufacturer OUI and a 24-bit unique number.

61. What is the MAC broadcast address ?

Answer: FFFF:FFFF:FFFF

62. What are the two switch port types ?

Answer:

Access port and trunk port. The switch ports support static and dynamic assignment.

63. What is the purpose of the switch native VLAN ?

Answer:

It is used to forward untagged packets between switches. In addition Layer 2 control plane traffic such as VTP, CDP, DTP, and PAgP protocols is always sent across native VLAN. The default is VLAN 1 however can be assigned to something else. The native VLAN must match between connected switches. In addition the native VLAN for switch trunk interfaces should not be assigned to VLAN 1 to prevent STP issues.

64. What command configures an access port on a switch with VLAN 3 ?

Answer:

Re-assign the port to a new VLAN if you delete the current VLAN assignment.

switch# **interface** [interface]
switch(config-if)# **switchport mode access**
switch(config-if)# **switchport access vlan 3**

65. What command lists all VLANs configured on a Catalyst switch ?

Answer:

router# **show vlan** [brief]

66. How do you configure a trunk port on a switch ?

Answer:

switch(config)# **interface** [interface]
switch(config-if)# **switchport mode trunk**
switch(config-if)# **encapsulation dot1q**

67. What is the purpose of Dynamic Trunking Protocol (DTP) ?

Answer:

The DTP protocol will negotiate a dynamic trunk link between 2 switches based on each neighbor port settings. The Cisco switch trunk link must support at least Fast Ethernet (100 Mbps) speed. The other option is static configuration where trunk interface is configured with **switchport nonegotiate** command.

68. Configure switch to router trunking with VLAN 10 and VLAN 20 ?

Answer:

switch(config)# interface Gi0/1
switch(config-if)# **switchport access vlan** 10
switch(config-if)# **switchport mode access**
switch(config)# interface Gi0/2
switch(config-if)# **switchport access vlan** 10
switch(config-if)# **switchport mode access**

switch(config)# interface Gi0/3
switch(config-if)# **switchport access vlan** 20
switch(config-if)# **switchport mode access**

router(config)# **interface Gi0/0.10**
router(config-subif)# **encapsulation dot1q 10**
router(config-subif)# **ip address** [subinterface ip address] [sub mask]

router(config-subif)# **interface Gi0/0.20**
router(config-subif)# **encapsulation dot1q 20**
router(config-subif)# **ip address** [subinterface ip address] [sub mask]

69. What is the purpose of port security and commands to configure it ?

Answer:

The port security feature filters what desktop can connect to the switch port, number of devices and violation action.

switch# **config terminal**
switch(config)# **interface** [interface]
switch(config-if)# **switchport port-security**
switch(config-if)# **switchport port-security mac-address** [addr]

70. What is the default VLAN ?

Answer:

The default VLAN assigned to all switch ports is VLAN 1. The default for the native VLAN is VLAN 1 as well.

71. What is the Spanning Tree Protocol (STP) bridge ID ?

Answer:

The bridge ID is comprised of switch priority and MAC address.

72. How is the switch root bridge elected ?

Answer:

The switch with lowest bridge ID is elected. The lowest Bridge ID is selected from the switch with the lowest MAC address and priority value.

73. What are the 5 stages of STP convergence ?

Answer:

block, listen, learn, forward, disable

74. How is STP information sent between switches ?

Answer:

The BPDU is sent at 2 second intervals as a default. The BPDU types include Topology Change Notification (TCN), Topology Change Acknowledgement (TCA) and Configuration BPDU.

75. What is Portfast and where is it applied ?

Answer:

Enables immediate forwarding of packets at a switch access port. It is only suitable for access ports with desktops for instance or any device that should not participate is STP.

76. What is Portfast BPDUGuard and what command enables it ?

Answer:

STP enhancement with RSTP and RPVST+ applied to Portfast enabled switch ports. The switch port is err-disabled when a BPDU arrives and port is prevented from participating in spanning tree.

switch# **spanning-tree bpdugard enable**

77. What command will show spanning tree for a VLAN ?

Answer:

router# **show spanning-tree vlan** [vlan number]

78. Configure a port channel and assign a channel group to interface ?

Answer:

switch(config)# **interface port-channe**l [number]
switch(config-if)# **no switchport**
switch(config-if)# **ip address** [ip address] [subnet mask]

switch(config)# **interface** [interface]
switch(config-if)# **channel-group 1 mode on**

79. What is the purpose of a switch trunk ?

Answer:

The trunk forwards multiple VLANs across a switch link ?

80. What is 802.1q ?

Answer:

It is the Cisco default trunk encapsulation for tagging packets with VLAN membership.

81. Where is IOS Code stored on a router or switch ?

Answer:

Flash memory

82. Where is the configuration script stored ?

Answer:

NVRAM

83. What memory is used for running IOS code ?

Answer:

DRAM

84. What 3 modes are available with VTP ?

Answer:

Client, server and transparent.

85. What is the default VTP mode for Catalyst switches ?

Answer:

Server mode.

86. What are the 3 VTP advertisement types ?

Answer:

Summary advertisements (5 minutes) - VTP domain name and the configuration revision number. Switch compares the configuration revision to its own revision for each VTP domain. The packet is dropped if the switch revision number is equal or higher. If lower, an advertisement request is sent.

Subset Advertisement – Any VLAN changes to a switch enabled as a VTP server will increment the switch configuration revision number. The switch then issues a summary advertisement.

Advertisement Requests - occurs when there is a switch reboot, VTP domain name change or switch receives summary with higher configuration revision number.

87. What occurs when a switch gets a VTP advertisement from a different VTP domain ?

Answer:

The switch drops such an advertisement

88. What cable type is used for switch to switch connectivity ?

Answer:

Cross-over cable

IP Addressing

89. What is CIDR notation for default Class A, B and C subnet masks ?

Answer:

Class A = 255.255.255.0 (/8)
Class B = 255.255.0.0 (/16)
Class C = 255.255.255.0 (/24)

90. Name host, network and broadcast address for 192.168.34.7 /28 ?

Answer:

host address = 192.168.34.1 (hosts available = 1-254)
network address = 192.168.34.0
broadcast address = 192.168.34.15

91. What is the zero subnet ?

Answer:

The zero subnet would enable 192.168.34.0 and provides an additional available subnet.

92. What is the purpose of NAT ?

Answer:

It allows connectivity to the internet while deploying private IP addressing to their network. The private IP addressing is translated to a public routable IP address at the router or firewall.

93. What are default subnet masks for Class A, B and C IP addressing ?

Answer:

Class A = 255.0.0.0
Class B = 255.255.0.0
Class C = 255.255.255.0

94. What is the network and broadcast address for 10.100.34.1 /24 ?

Answer:

The subnet mask determines the network address and broadcast address and not the default subnet mask.

network address = 10.100.34.0
broadcast address = 10.100.34.255

95. How do you summarize 172.16.0.0 to 172.16.40.0 (41 subnets) ?

Answer:

That requires summarizing at least 64 subnets for summarization on a classful boundary. The 64 bit boundary = 11000000 (172.16.192.0) to summarize from 172.16.0.0 - 172.16.63.0

WAN Protocols

96. What is Frame Relay CIR ?

Answer:

Committed Information Rate (CIR) is the average rate (bps) guaranteed by the Frame Relay service provider to a customer.

97. What are the two types of Frame Relay encapsulation ?

Answer:

Cisco (proprietary) and IETF (open standard) for multi-vendor connectivity.

98. What are the key features of any VPN ?

Answer:

Confidentiality, integrity, authentication and anti-replay protection for data.

99. What is the TCP three-way handshake ?

Answer:

Establishes a connection from source to destination using the SYN and ACK flags in the Code Bits section of the TCP header. The source starts the three-way handshake by sending a TCP header to the destination with the SYN flag set. The destination responds back with the SYN and ACK flag sent. The destination uses the received sequence number plus 1 as the Acknowledgement number. The source responds back with only the ACK bit set then data sent.

100. What are the TCP port assignments for the following applications ?

Answer:

FTP (Control)	TCP 21
SSH	TCP 22
Telnet	TCP 23
SMTP	TCP 25
DNS	TCP, UDP 53
TFTP	UDP 69
HTTP	TCP 80
HTTPS	TCP 443

Bibliography

Catalyst 3750 Software Upgrade in a stack configuration with Use of the Command-Line Interface, Configuration Examples and Tech Notes, Cisco Systems, 2009

Working with Cisco IOS XE Software Bundles, System Management Configuration Guide, Cisco IOS XE Release 3SE (Catalyst 3650 Switches), Cisco Systems, 2013

3850 Switch IOS XE upgrade detail (standalone), Cisco Support Community, 2015

Catalyst 3850 Series Switch Upgrade, Management, and Recovery Techniques, Troubleshooting Tech Notes, Cisco Systems, 2014

Configuring Cisco License Call Home, Cisco Systems 2008

Cisco Catalyst 3650 Series Switches, Q&A, Cisco Systems 2014

Cisco IOS XE Software for Cisco ASR 1000 Series Routers Product Bulletin, Cisco Systems 2012

Cisco IOS Configuration Fundamentals Command Reference, Release 12.2, Cisco Systems 2006

Troubleshooting, Catalyst 3750-X and 3560-X Switch Software Configuration Guide, Release 12.2(53)SE2 Cisco Systems

Password Recovery Procedure for Cisco NX-OS, Cisco Systems, 2012

Difficulty upgrading IOS on 3750 switch and stack, Cisco Support Community, 2011

Catalyst 3750 Software Upgrade in a stack configuration with use of command-line interface, Configuration examples and tech notes, Cisco Systems, 2009

How to upgrade a Cisco stack, CiscoZine, 2014

Cisco IOS Interface Command Reference, Release 12.2, Cisco Systems 2006

Catalyst 3750 Command Reference, Release 12.2(55)SE, Cisco Systems 2010

Cisco IOS Software Release 15 M and T Features and Hardware Support, Cisco Systems 2009

Understanding Cisco IOS Naming Conventions, John Rullan, Cisco Systems 2005

White Paper: Cisco IOS and NX-OS Software Reference Guide, Cisco Systems

Upgrading Software Images on Catalyst 6000/6500 Series Switches, Configuration examples and tech notes, Cisco Systems, 2009

Cisco IOS Software Packaging 12.2SX, Q&A, Cisco Systems, 2011

Cisco Catalyst 6500 Enterprise Services Feature Set Software Image Upgrade Promotion, product bulletin, Cisco Systems 2008

Cisco's Integrated Services Routers Generation Two Licensing and Packaging, Cisco Systems 2012

Software Activation on Cisco ISR, Cisco ISR G2 and Cisco ISR 4K, Cisco Systems 2014

Cisco 3750-X and Cisco 3560-X Switch Features, Comparison and FAQs, Cisco Systems 2013

Cisco IOS Software Packaging and Licensing for the Cisco Catalyst 3750-E, 3560-E, 3750-X, and 3560-X Series Switches White Paper, Cisco Systems 2010

Cisco IOS Software Release 15M&T Q&A, Cisco Systems 2010

Cisco IOS Software Reference Guide White Paper, Cisco Systems 2012

Password Recovery Procedure for the Cisco Catalyst Fixed Configuration Layer 2 and Layer 3 Switches, Cisco Systems 2014

Licensing on 2960/3500/3750, Cisco Support Community 2011

Index

www.ingramcontent.com/pod-product-compliance
Lightning Source LLC
Chambersburg PA
CBHW080534060326
40690CB00022B/5123